Carlos Marrero

Wake Up Romeo

Tips to Rekindle Your Romantic Life

♥

Green Candy Press

Wake up Romeo
by Carlos Marrero
ISBN 1-931160-26-0
Published by Green Candy Press
www.greencandypress.com

Copyright © 2004 by Carlos Marrero.

All rights reserved. No part of this book may be reproduced in any form without written permission from the publisher, except by a reviewer, who may quote brief passages in a review where appropriate credit is given; nor may any part of this book be reproduced, stored in a retrieval system, or transmitted in any form or by any means—electronic, photocopying, recording, or other—without specific written permission from the publisher.

Design: Ian Phillips
Author photograph © Jim Cox, www.jimcox.net

All of the characters in this book are fictitious, and any resemblance to actual persons, living or dead, is purely coincidental.

Printed in China.
Massively Distributed by P.G.W.

❤️

To the beautiful souls that I have shared romantic experiences with, my Romeos. I am thankful for the lessons and the blessings that you brought into my life; without you I would have nothing to write about.

To Dan, for your caring, beautiful soul and unconditional love. I am so happy to call you my best friend. To Patrick, for your optimism and sense of youthfulness. To Raymond, for energizing my spiritual path. To Jeff, for the growing and the laughter. To ZVI, you are a true ROMEO!

To my brother Angel and his partner Tom, for being an inspiration; after sixteen years together and two beautiful kids, I applaud you.

But most of all I dedicate this book to the Romeo that lives in each of you. Perhaps he is asleep or just needs a nudge to come out, play, and fall in love all over again.

Wake Up!

Tips to rekindle your Romantic Life

♥ # Romance,

the elusive spark that exists at the beginning of a relationship, can all too often fizzle out over time. We may get wrapped up in so many distractions that we forget the most important thing in our relationship. To keep the fire burning. Creativity, timing, understanding his yearnings, and the element of surprise are some of the secrets to keeping the coals hot!

♥

We spend most of our lives searching for the one; then we get him and after a few years, or maybe even months, we start complaining about the lack of romance in the relationship. After hearing so many stories in this vein from my friends, and experiencing a few relationships myself, I decided to put my ideas and drawings into this book.

♥

❤

Wake up Romeo contains creative, thoughtful, sensual, ingenious and even some old-fashioned ideas (with a modern twist) that will help you (or him) keep or rekindle the spark back in your relationship.

❤

Some of these ideas will work for both the infatuation stage and the burning passion of a long-term relationship. Take the time and effort to take your relationship to the next level and deepen your love life. It is also wise to carry out these gestures from a loving heart—without ❤ expectations. Keep an open mind and a willing spirit to try new things. You will not only surprise your sweetheart, but also yourself.

Now You're Cookin'

After a few nights of fab restaurants and getting to know each other, you'll have to start working your magic. Mama always told me, "The way to a man's heart is through his stomach." Learn how to cook his favorite meal and surprise him with it one night. Or for you kitchen-challenged Romeos—order takeout and cleverly disguise it as a homemade meal!

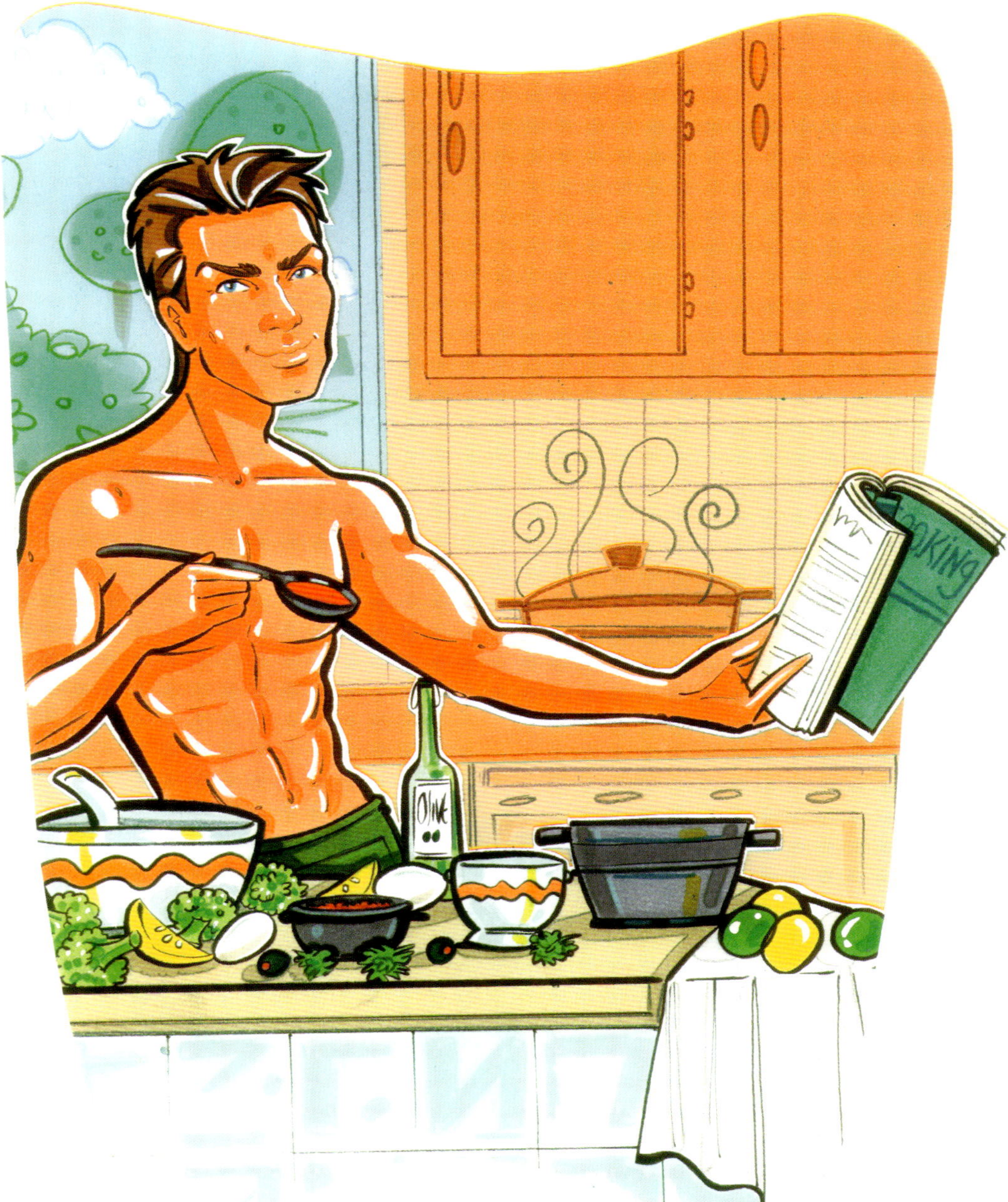
Olive

Nice Basket

The first time your Romeo spends the night, have a basket of goodies waiting on the bed for him. Suggested items could be a new toothbrush, razor, shaving gel, scented soap, bubble bath, lotions, and a rubber ducky. He'll feel welcome and at home in no time.

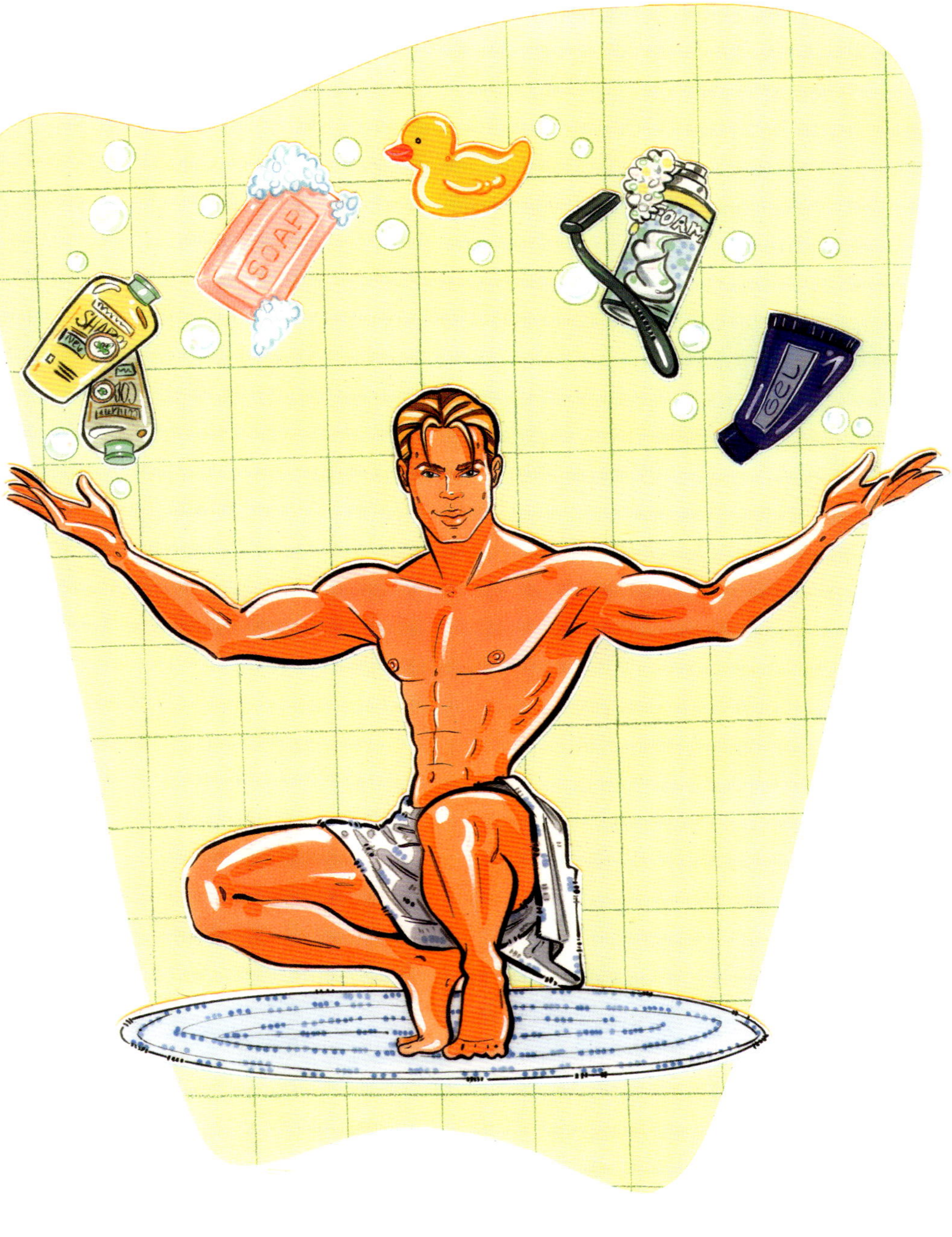
SOAP
GEL

They're Playing Our Song

Try to remember what song was playing, or was popular when you first met. Make it your theme song. Dance to it together under the stars or in the living room. Soon, whenever you and your Romeo hear it, he can't help but want to be in your arms.

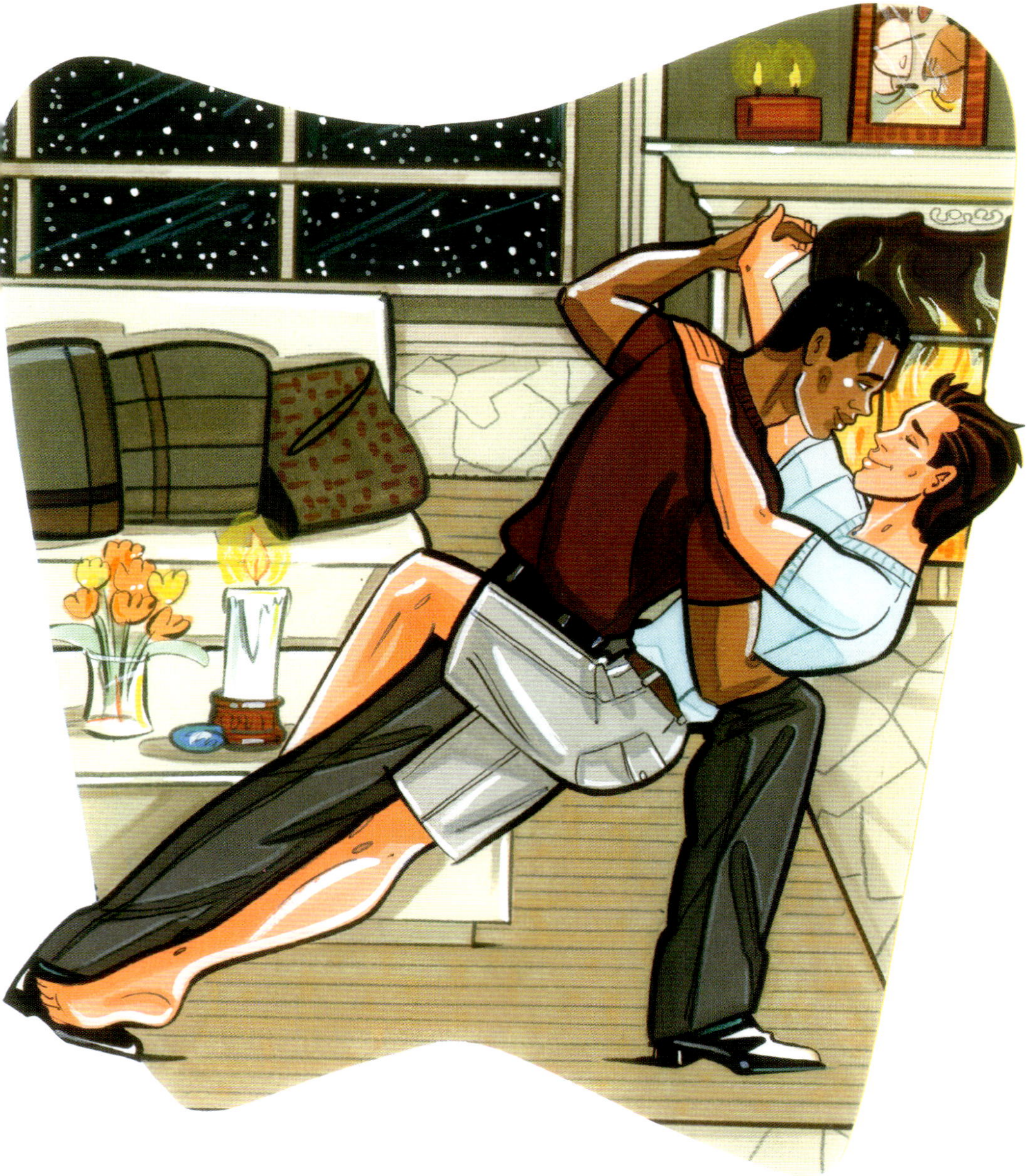

Romeo's List

Take the time to sit down and write down all of his good qualities, then read them to him while looking into his eyes. (You are allowed to stretch the truth a little). By the time you are done reading, you will have quickly moved to the top of his list.

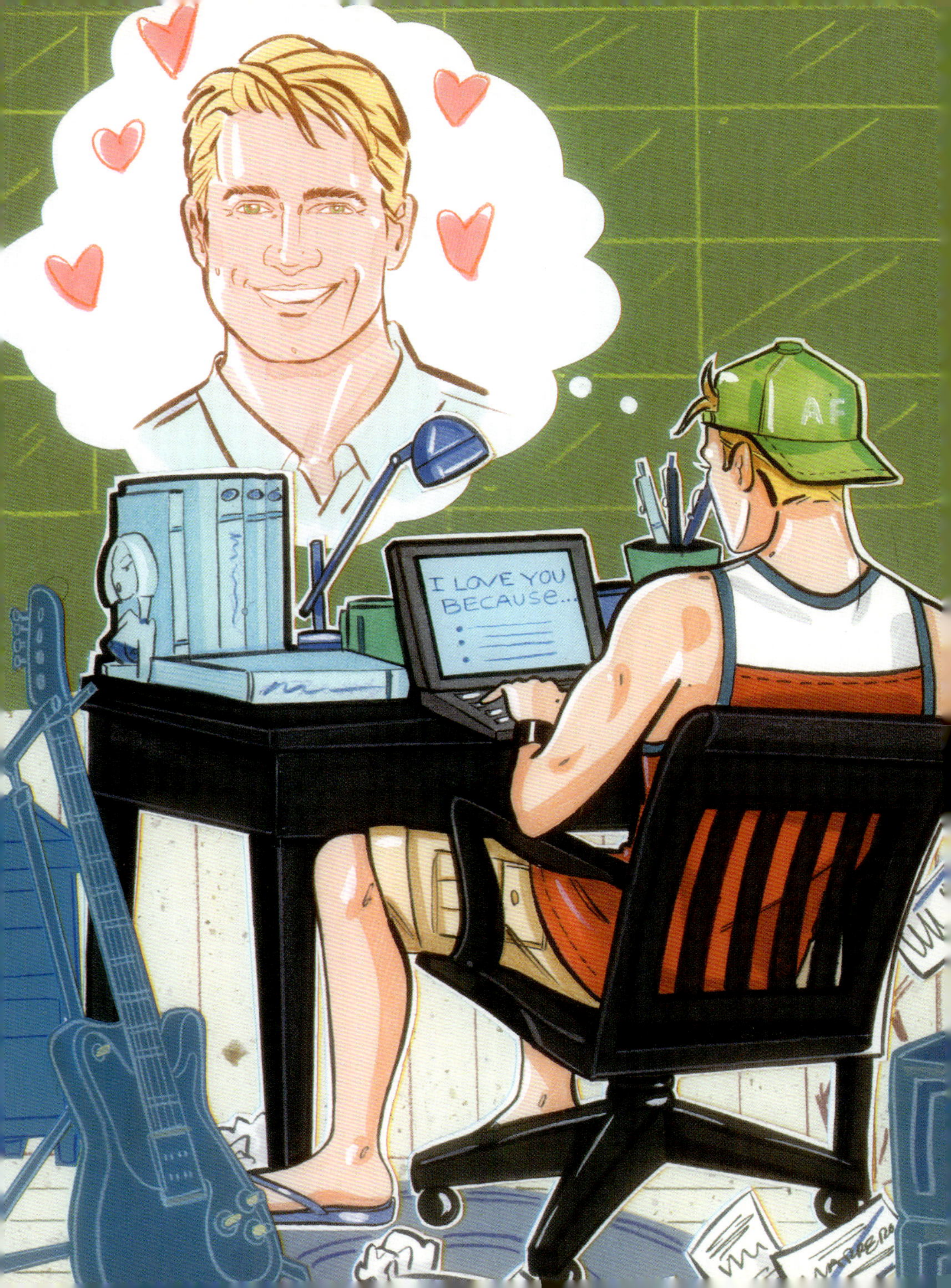
I LOVE YOU
BECAUSE...

Doggy Style

If your Romeo has a pet—a cat, dog, or something more exotic—understand that his "best friend" is a priority to him. Share your love by casually surprising your Romeo's pet with a treat and you will win extra romance points. And you might not have to "beg" later.

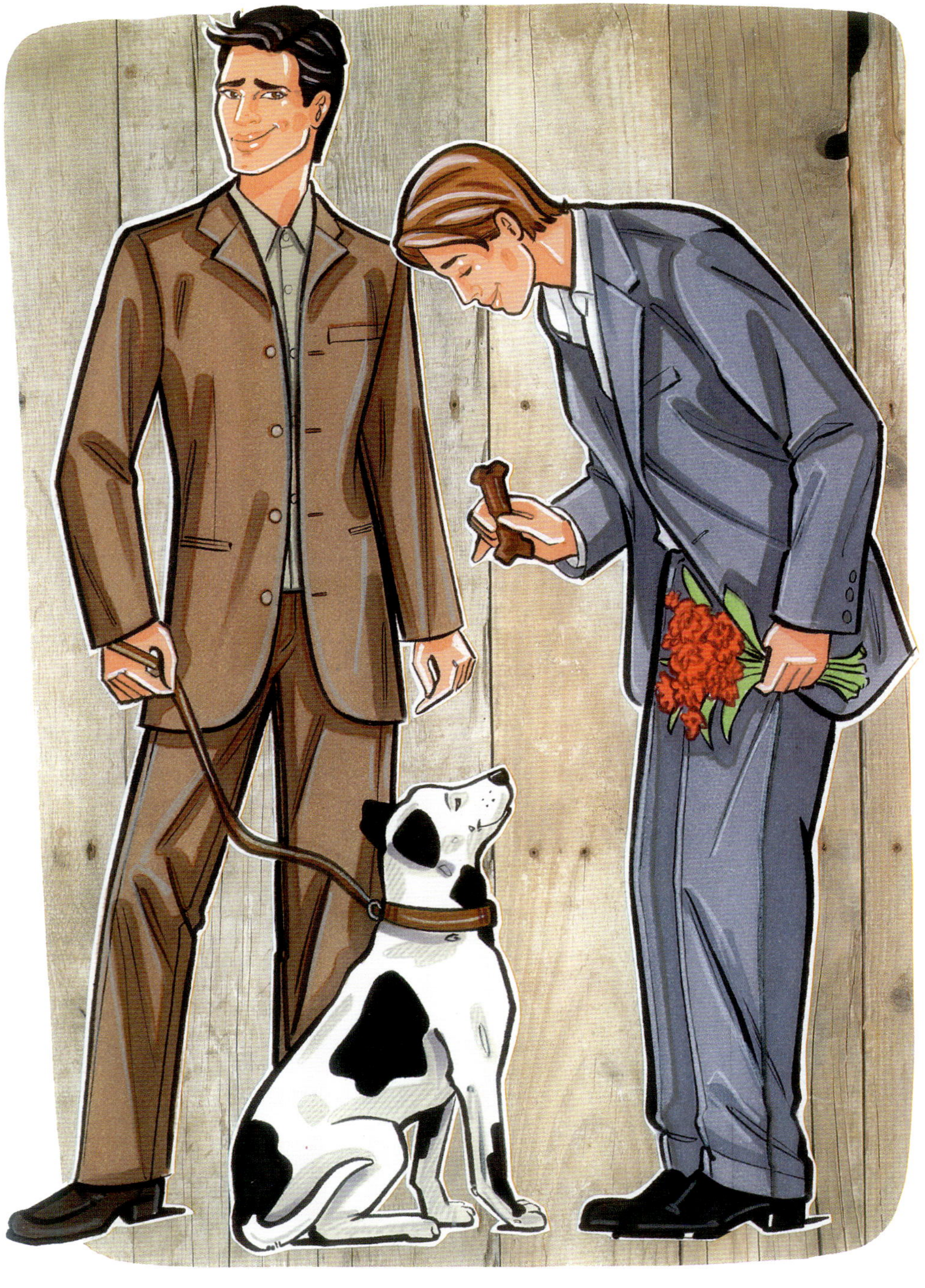

Emergency Kit: Why Not?

A true romantic is always prepared to be spontaneous. Organize a box with simple essentials for an "impromptu" romantic moment. This way you aren't running around your house looking for what you need and finding that the mood has already left you or him.

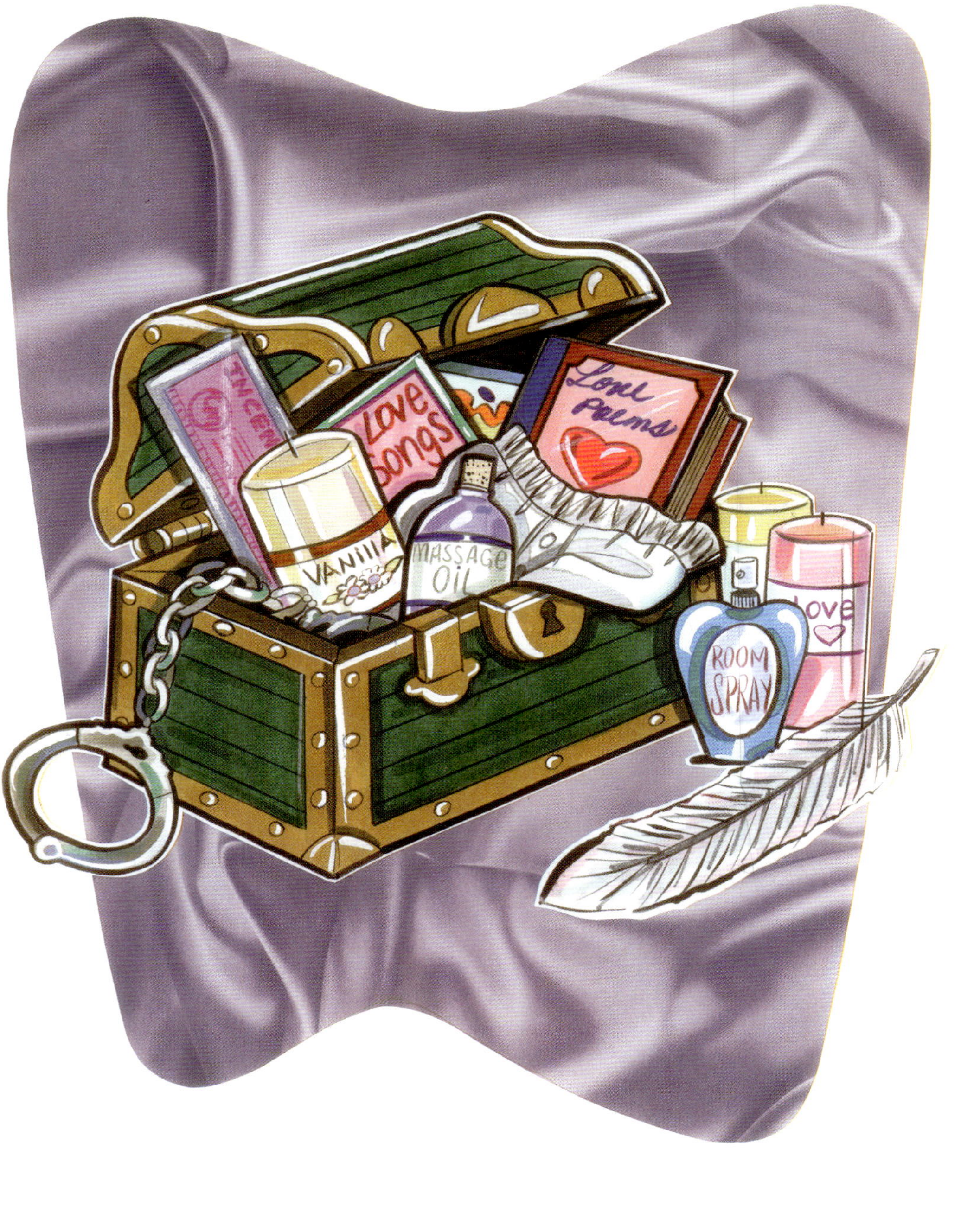
Love Songs
Love Poems
VANILLA
MASSAGE OIL
ROOM SPRAY
Love

Clean Up Your Act!

Throw away those old T-shirts that he hates. Go buy some new ones that he's sure to like on you.

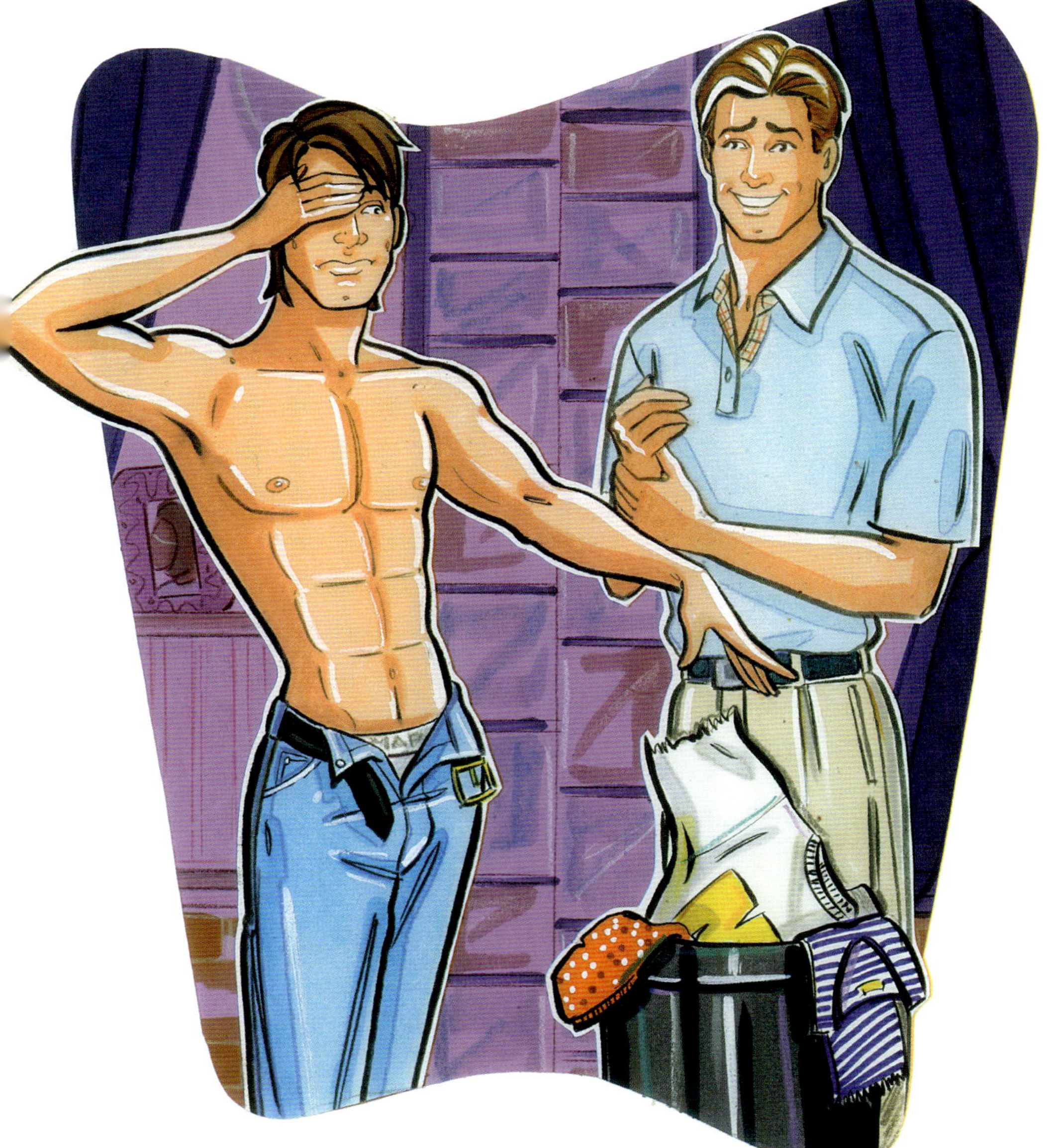

YEEHAAAH!

Sometimes it's all about trying something new. Dinner, movies, or the theater can be romantic, but sometimes too much of a good thing can be as fatal as a rattlesnake bite. Break the mold. Think out of the box. Try attending a gay rodeo, go kayaking, learn pottery painting, take line dancing classes. The memories you'll share in experiencing these new adventures together could lead to many happy trails!

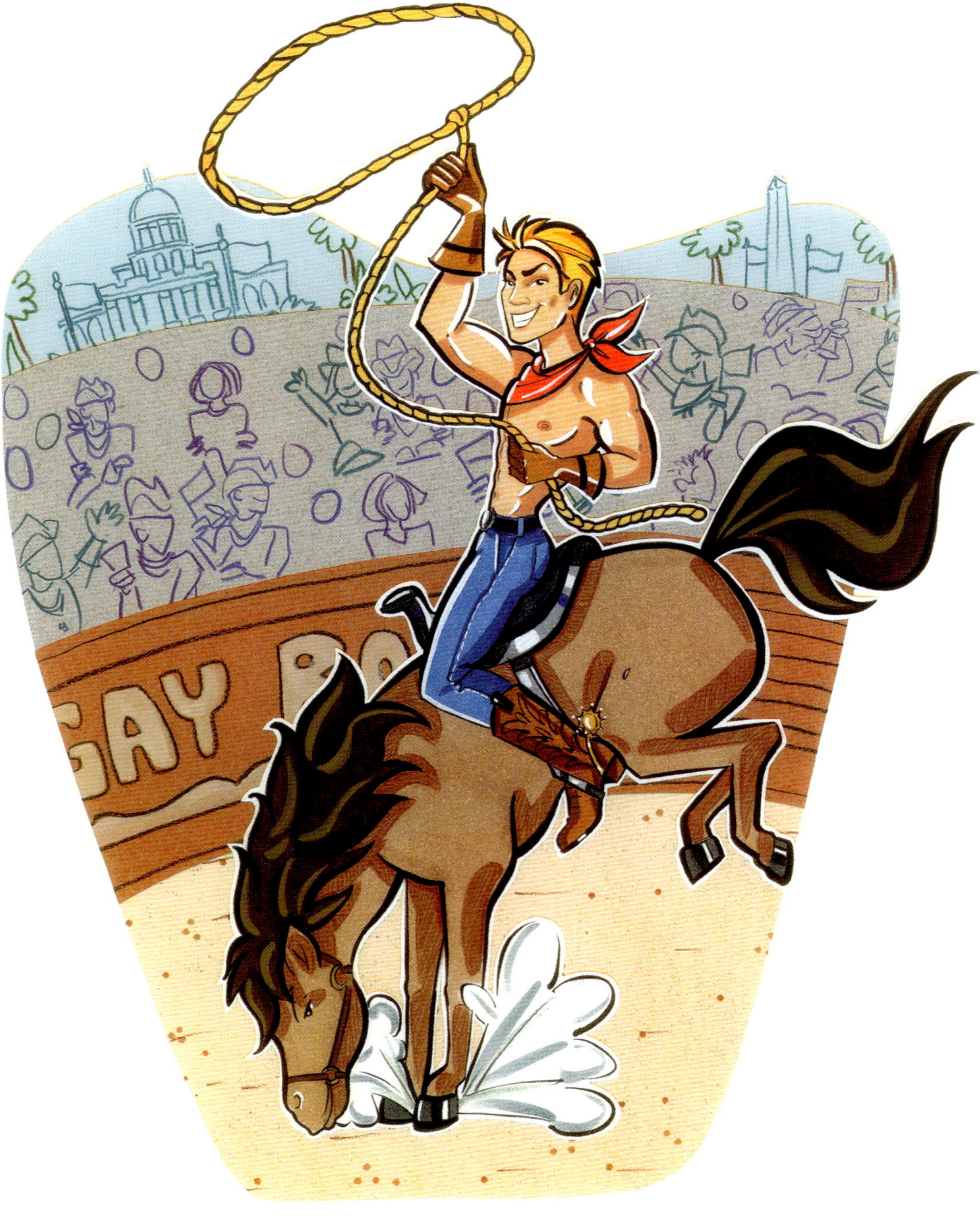
GAY

Pleasure Trail: Sex Marks the Spot!

Create a sexy scavenger hunt. When he comes home, have the lights turned off and candles lit throughout the house. Leave little instructional notes or clues for him to follow ending up in the bedroom or somewhere unexpected. You'll be waiting and ready with the treasure.

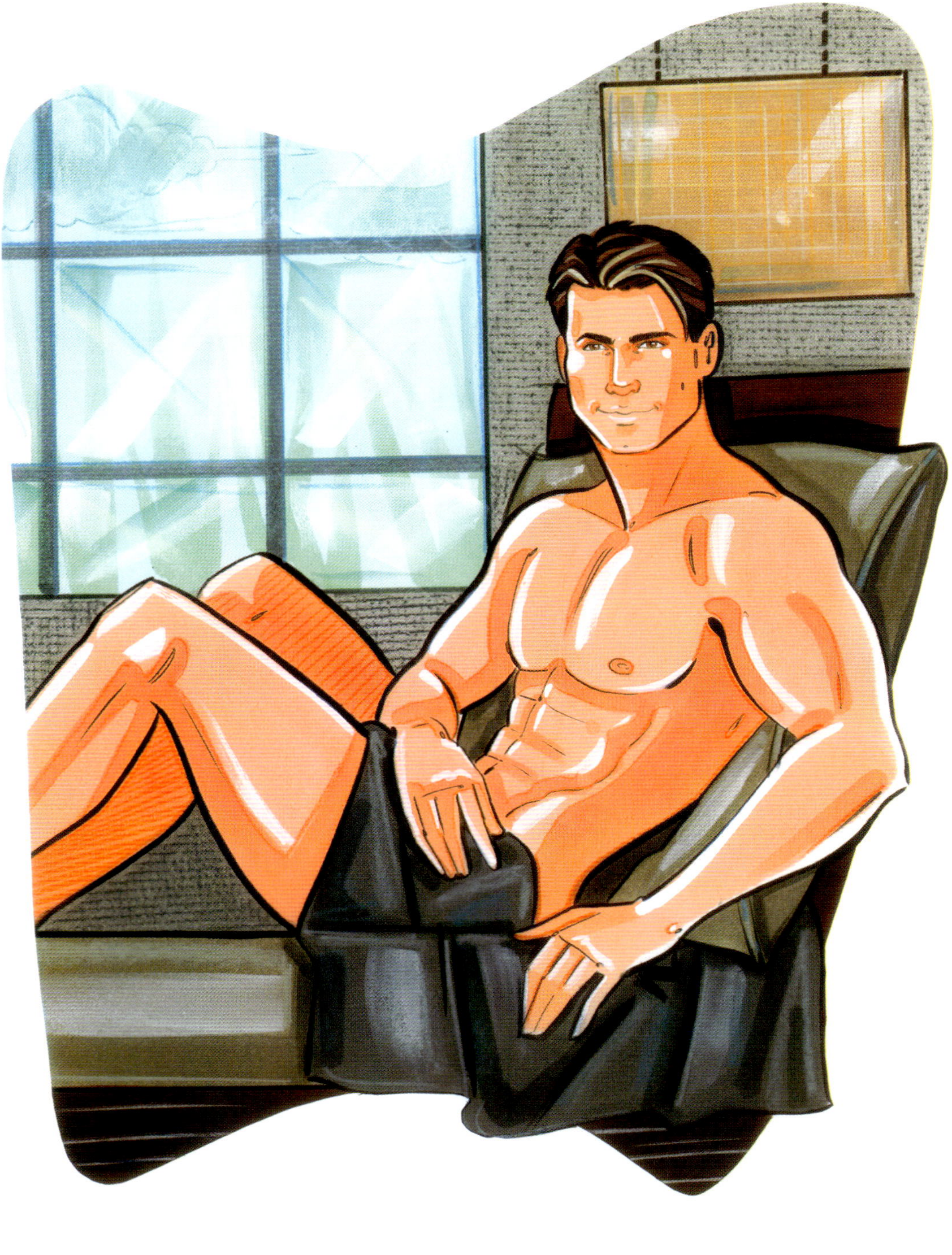

Lose Control

You'll find your Romeo less remote,
when you give up control.

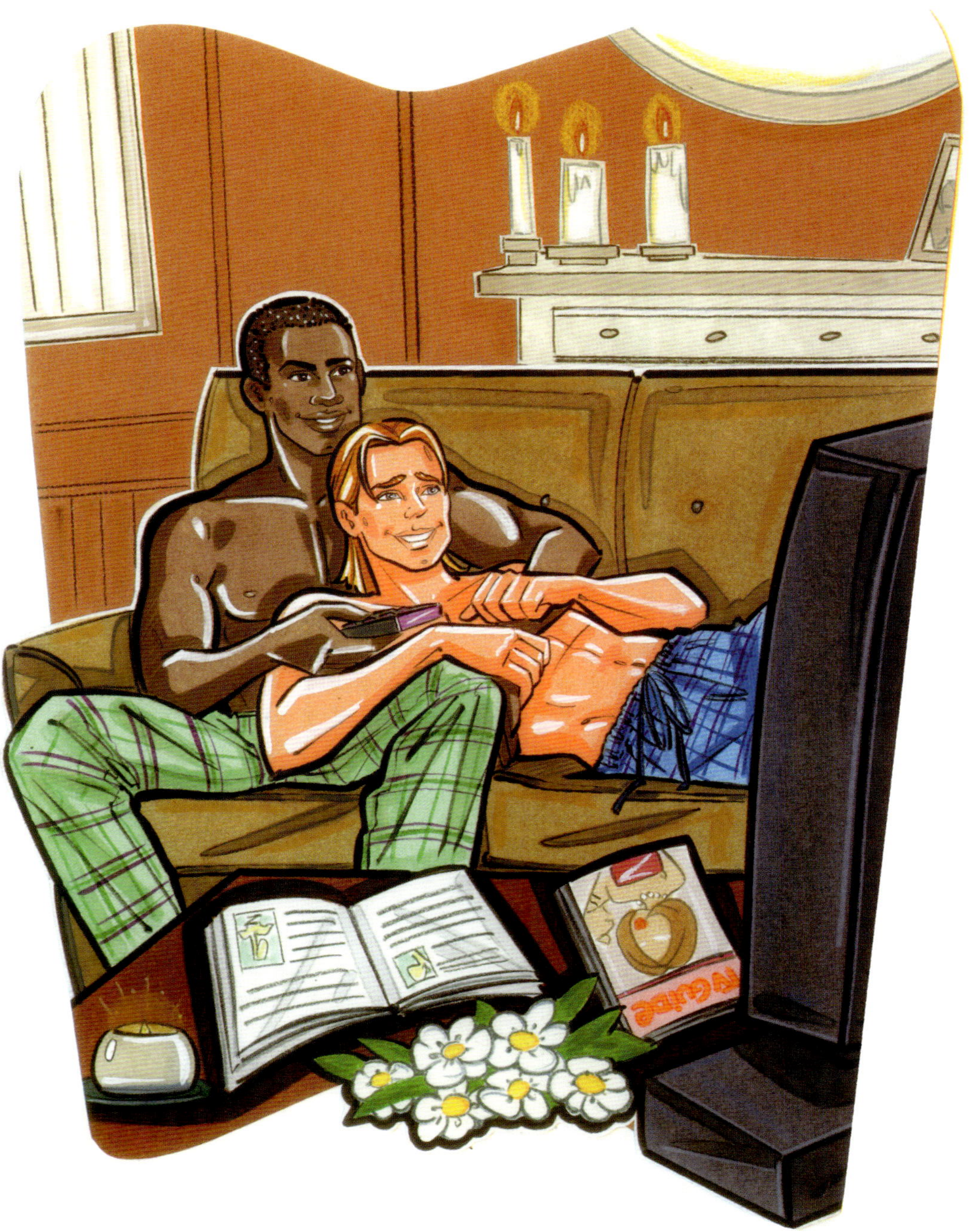

Budding Romance

Next Valentine's Day, send him eleven red roses and one white one. And write on the card, "You will always be my one-of-a-kind man."

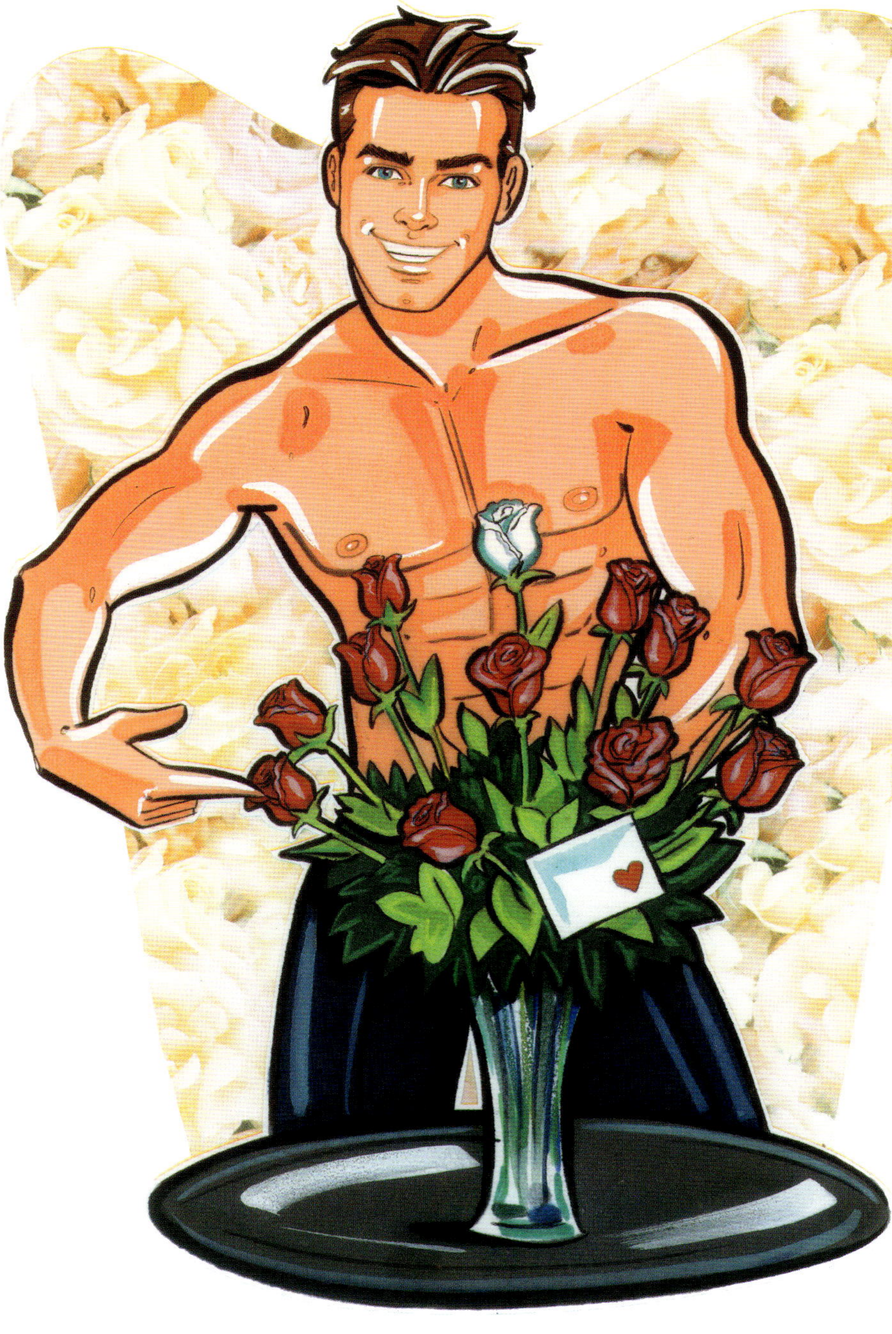

Is It Written in the Stars?

A visit to an astrologer or a psychic can add a sense of "knowing" to your relationship. It's fun and if you pick a good one, your reading can be full of surprises. I see easy days and hard nights ahead!

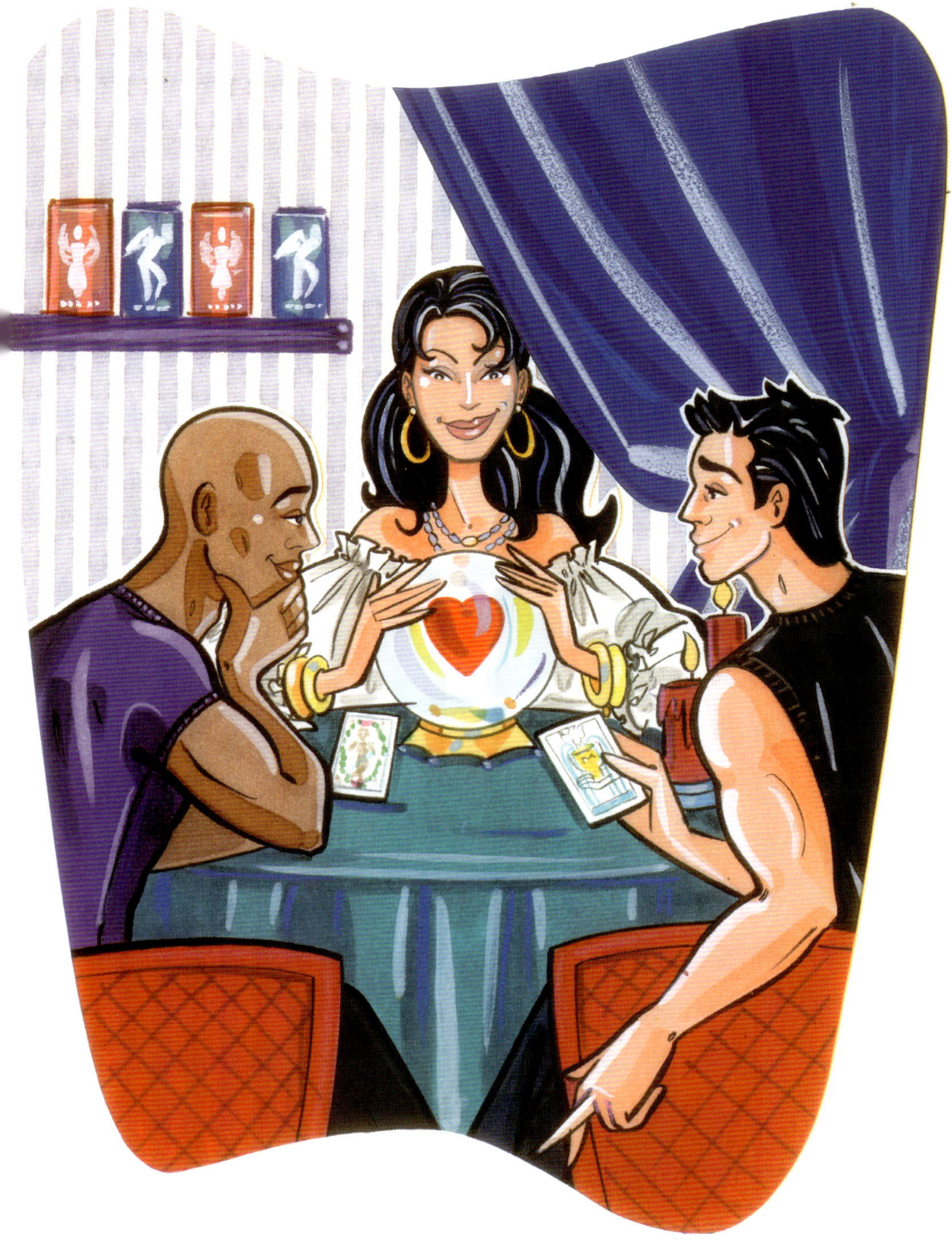

Mi Casa es Su Casa!

Nothing says things are going great better than giving him the key to your home. But give it to him in a creative way, like inside a balloon in a bouquet, or have it delivered to him at work and tell him to use it tonight. Or put it in a glass of champagne at your favorite restaurant. Even have it delivered to his house with a love note attatched. This won't just be his key to your house, but the key to his heart.

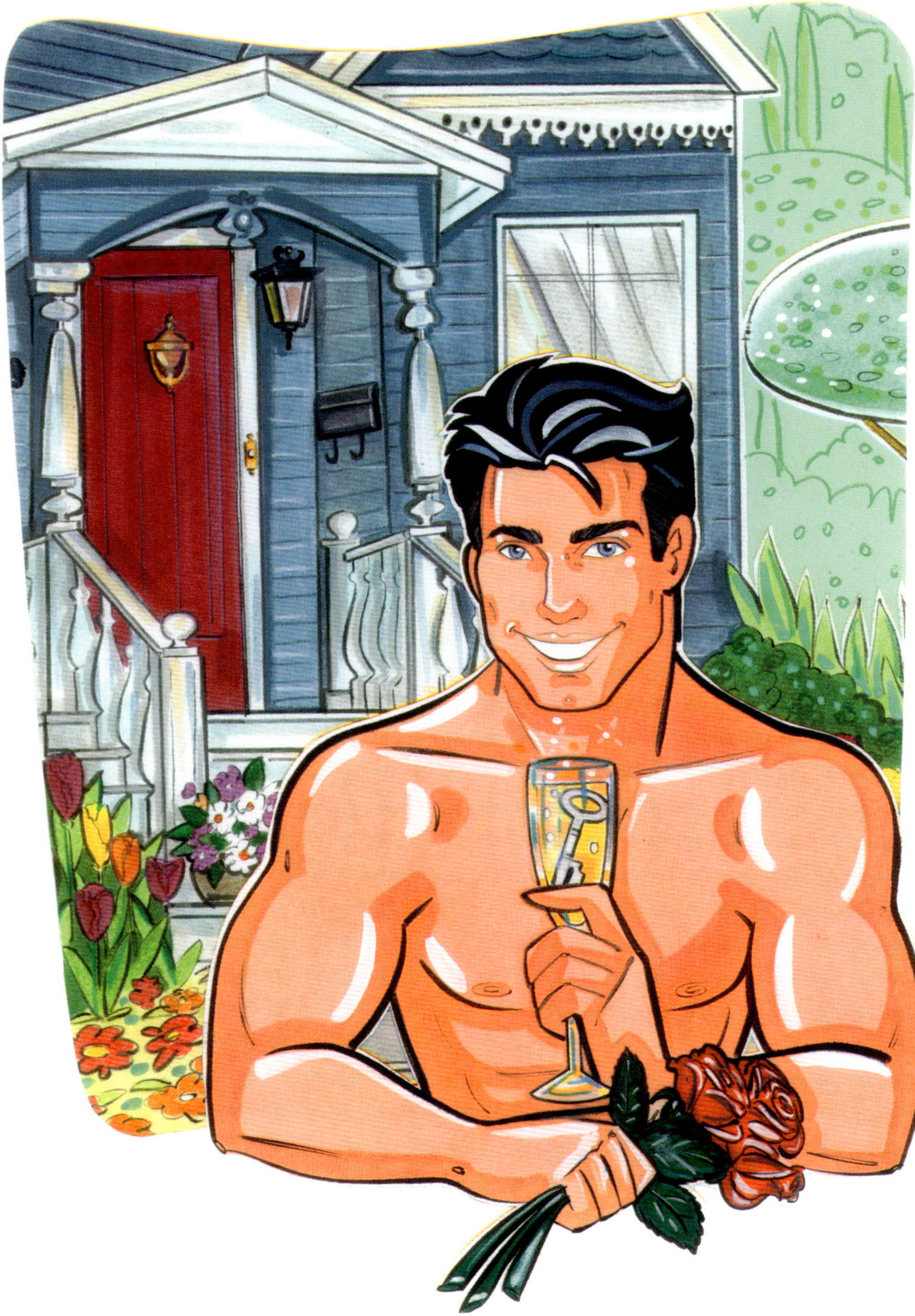

Fortune Teller

Next time you cook or order chinese food, carefully remove the fortunes from the fortune cookies with tweezers. Then make your own and reinsert them. Some examples might be: "You are eating with the man of your dreams," or "You will have the best sex of your life tonight." Remember, the sky's the limit!

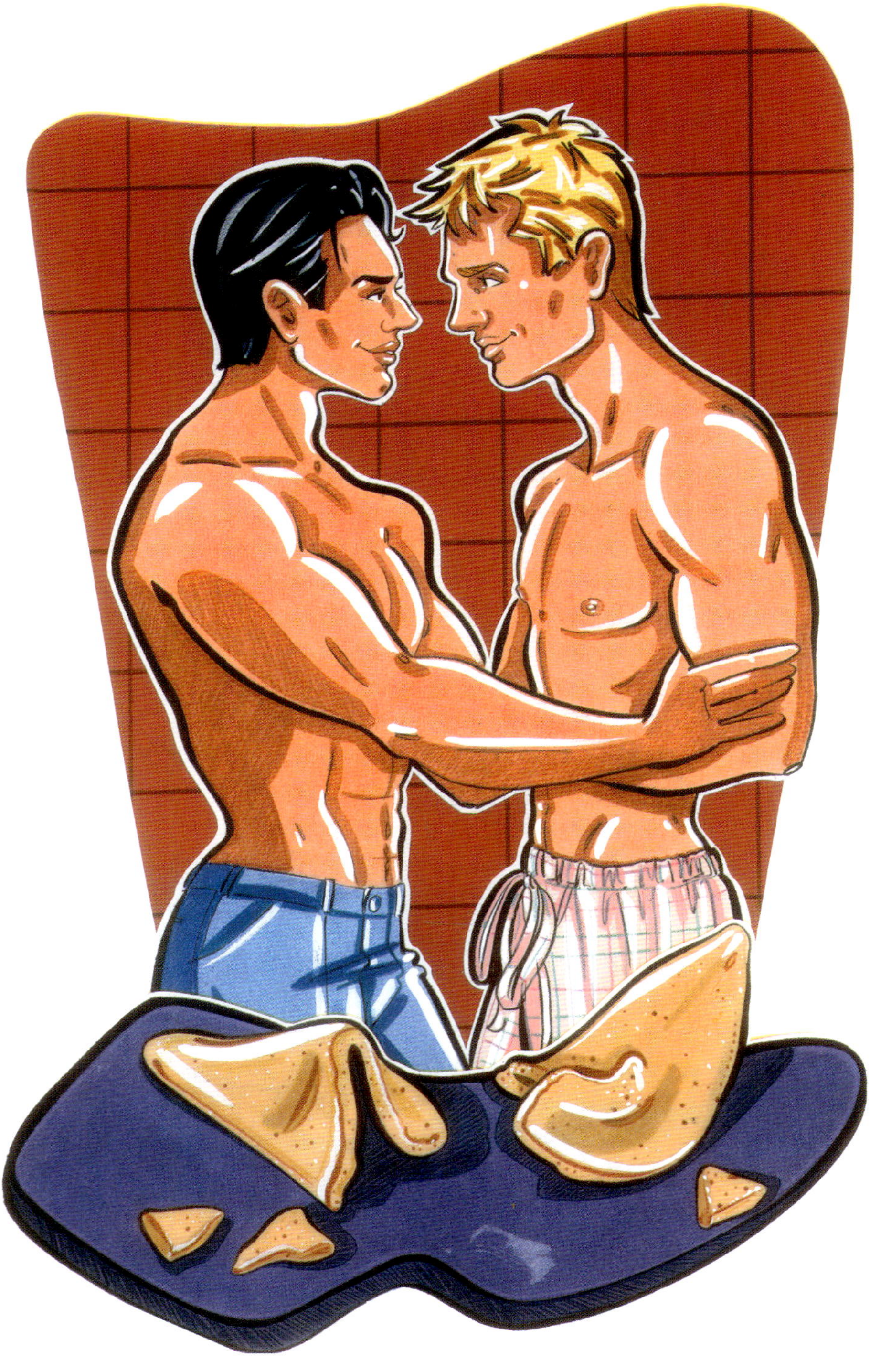

Give Him a Snow Job

Take your Romeo on a surprise ski weekend. There's just something about a day on the slopes. Having fun in the cold makes those nights by the fire or under the blankets much hotter.

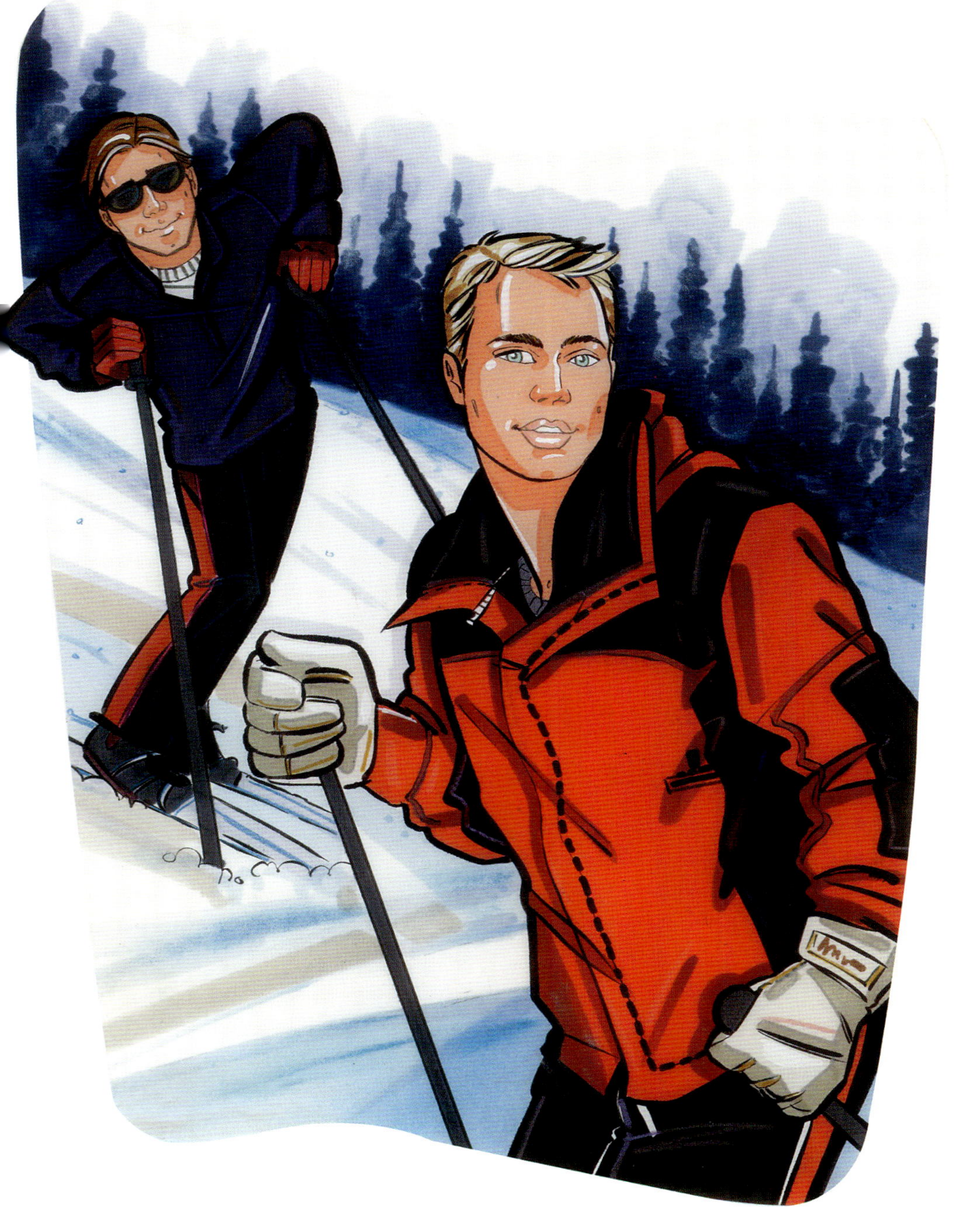

Make Your Own Rules

A fun, spontaneous game of strip poker or naked Twister could be just the thing to spice up a quiet night at home. Believe me, there are no losers when you play like this.

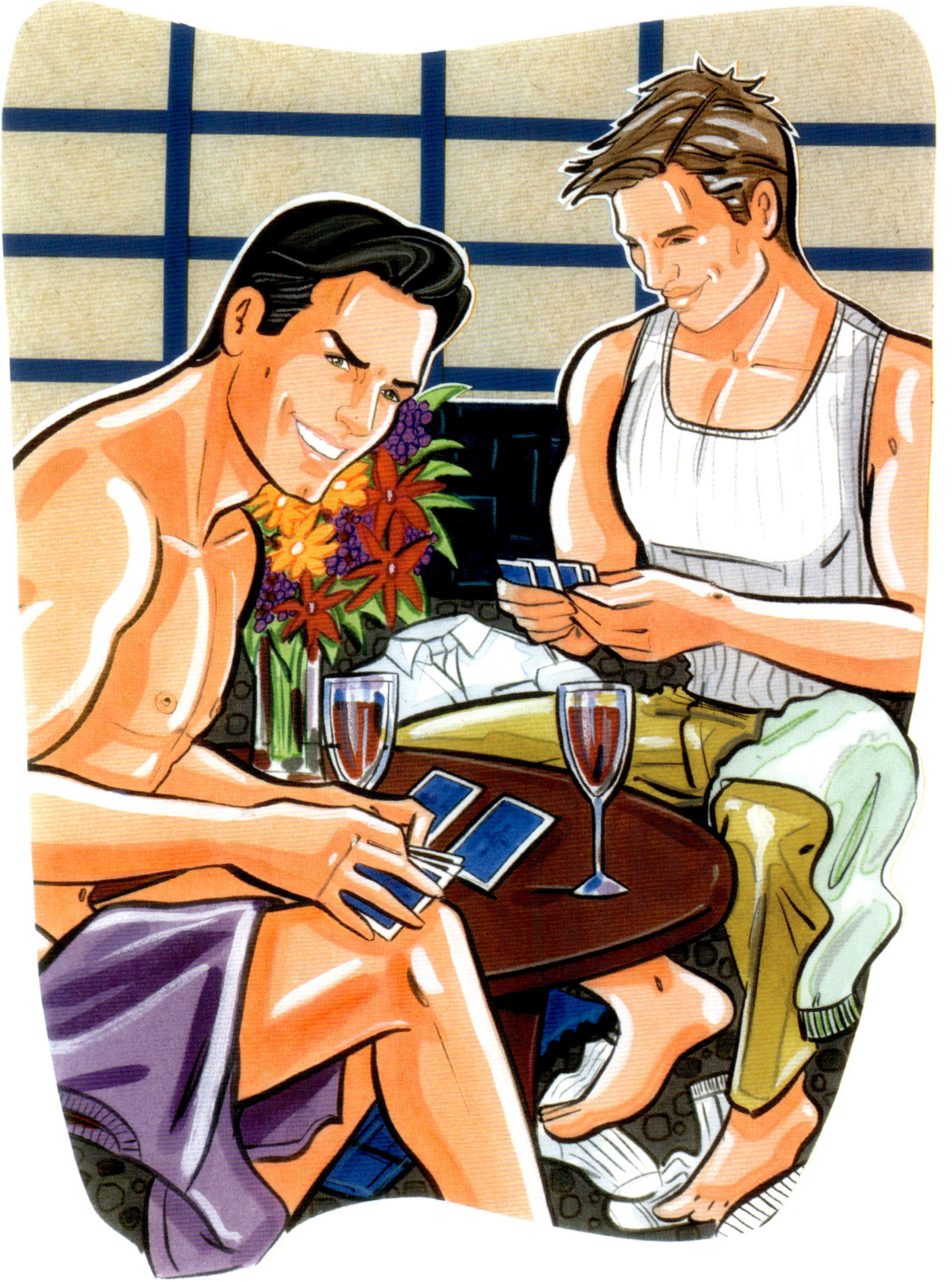

That's the Ticket!

Next time you plan to take him to a concert or show, buy the tickets, then go buy the CD soundtrack as well. Open it (at the store), insert the tickets, and then have the store shrink-wrap the CD again. When your Romeo opens the CD the tickets will fall out. I can hear the applause already—you might even get a standing ovation!

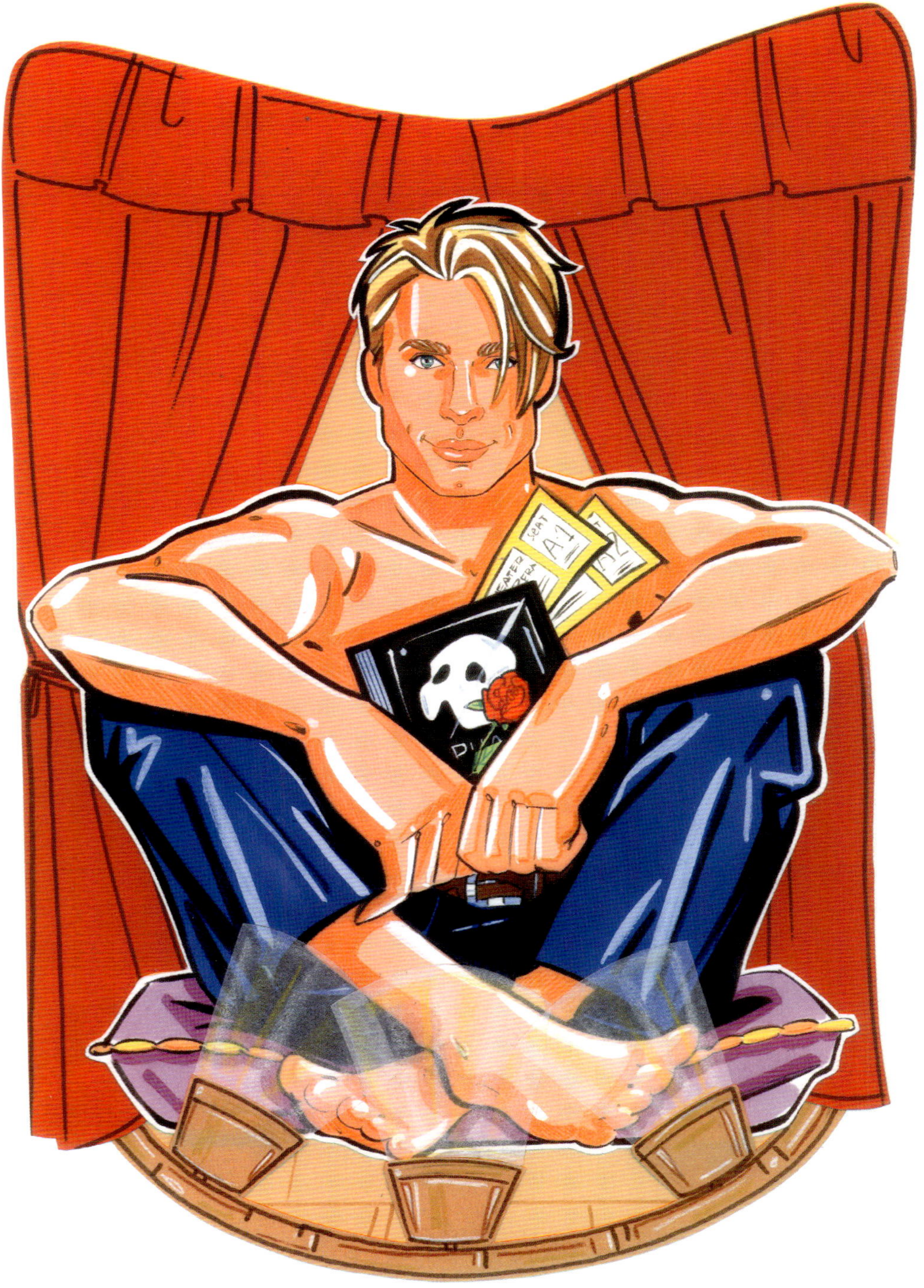
SEAT
A1

Musical Rooms

If you move into a new apartment, house or condo, christen it by making love in every room. You can do it all in one day, or a different room each day.

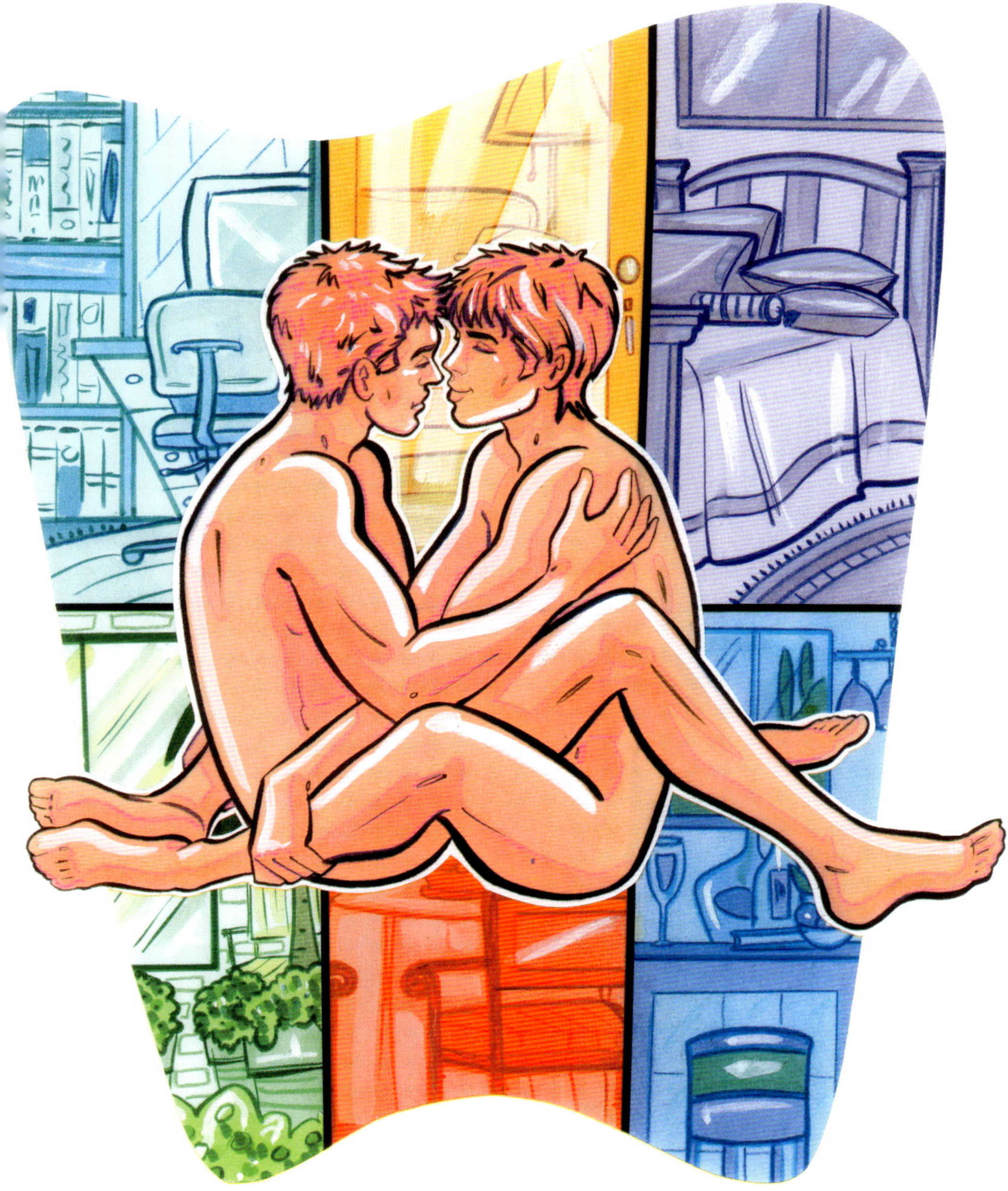

Wait!
I Have a Coupon For That

Okay, maybe it's not a new idea, but a book of coupons is still a great idea. It's up to you to make it special: everything from late night dog-walking to one night of position switching. The possibilities are endless. You can even have double coupon day. So get clippin'!

breakfast in BED
BOTTOM
CAR WASH
LAUNDRY
LAUNDRY
CAR WASH
chores
TOP
BACKRUB
CAR WAS

Remember When?

Remember the history you share together. Dust off those old photos, laugh at the then-trendy hairstyles and clothes, wonder whatever happened to so-and-so. A scrapbook is a fun project you can work on together and keep adding to as time goes on.

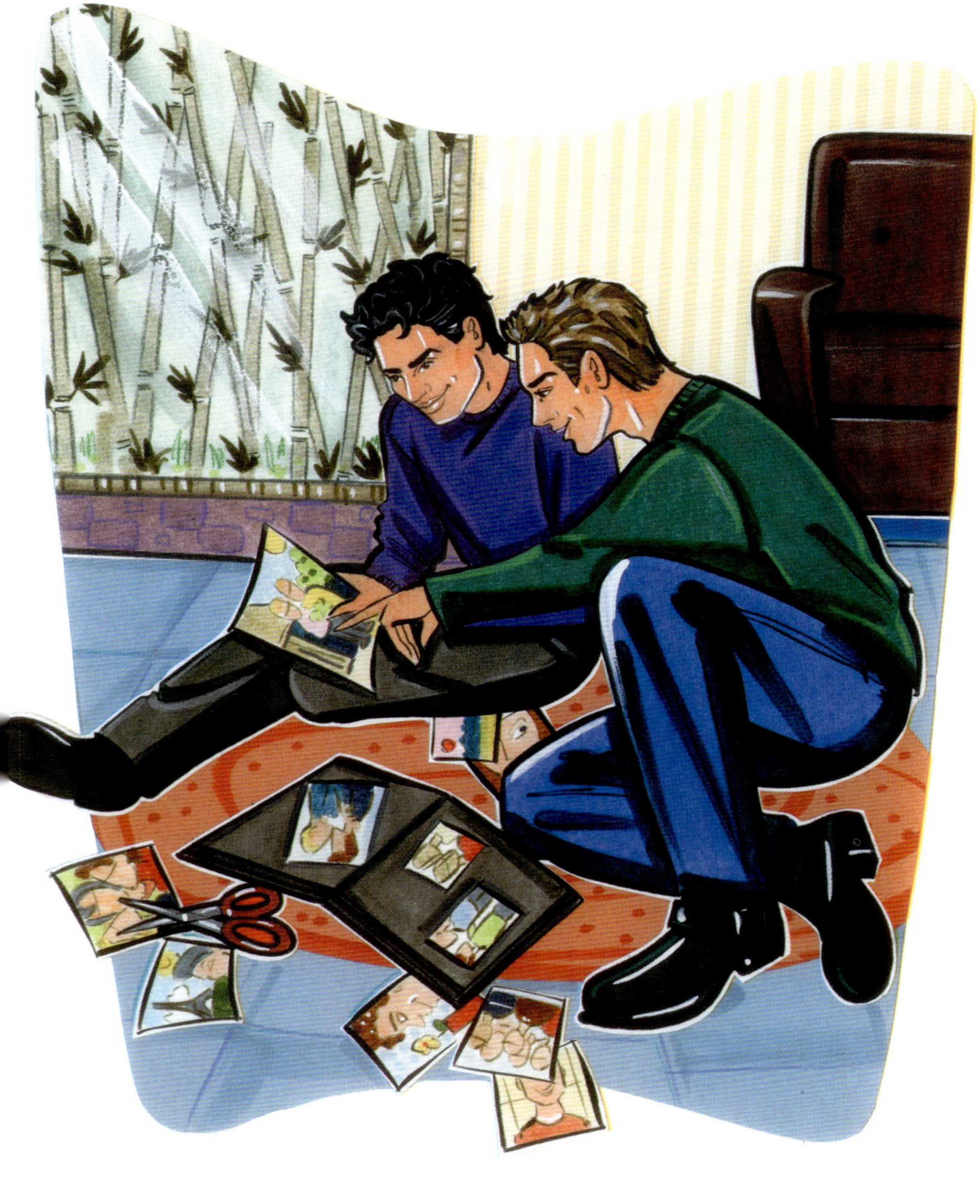

Role-Play!

Dressing up is a great way to add some spice to your sex life. Share your fantasies and become someone totally different. Even change your names for the situation. You might just give the performance of a lifetime.

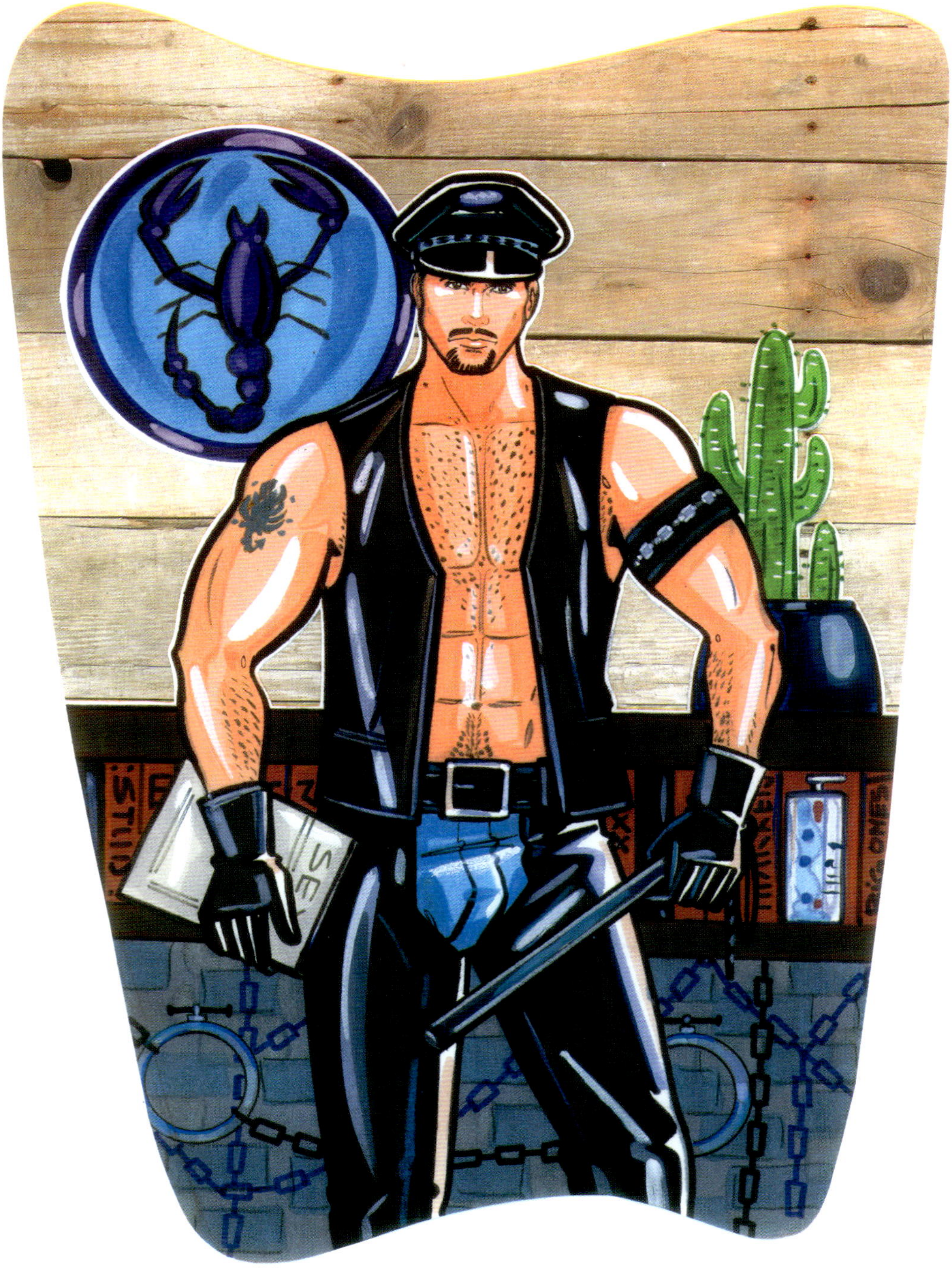
BIG ONES

It was a Very Good Year

On his birthday, buy a bottle of wine from the year he was born, and open it as a surprise. You can also find music, movies and magazines that date from the same time and share those.

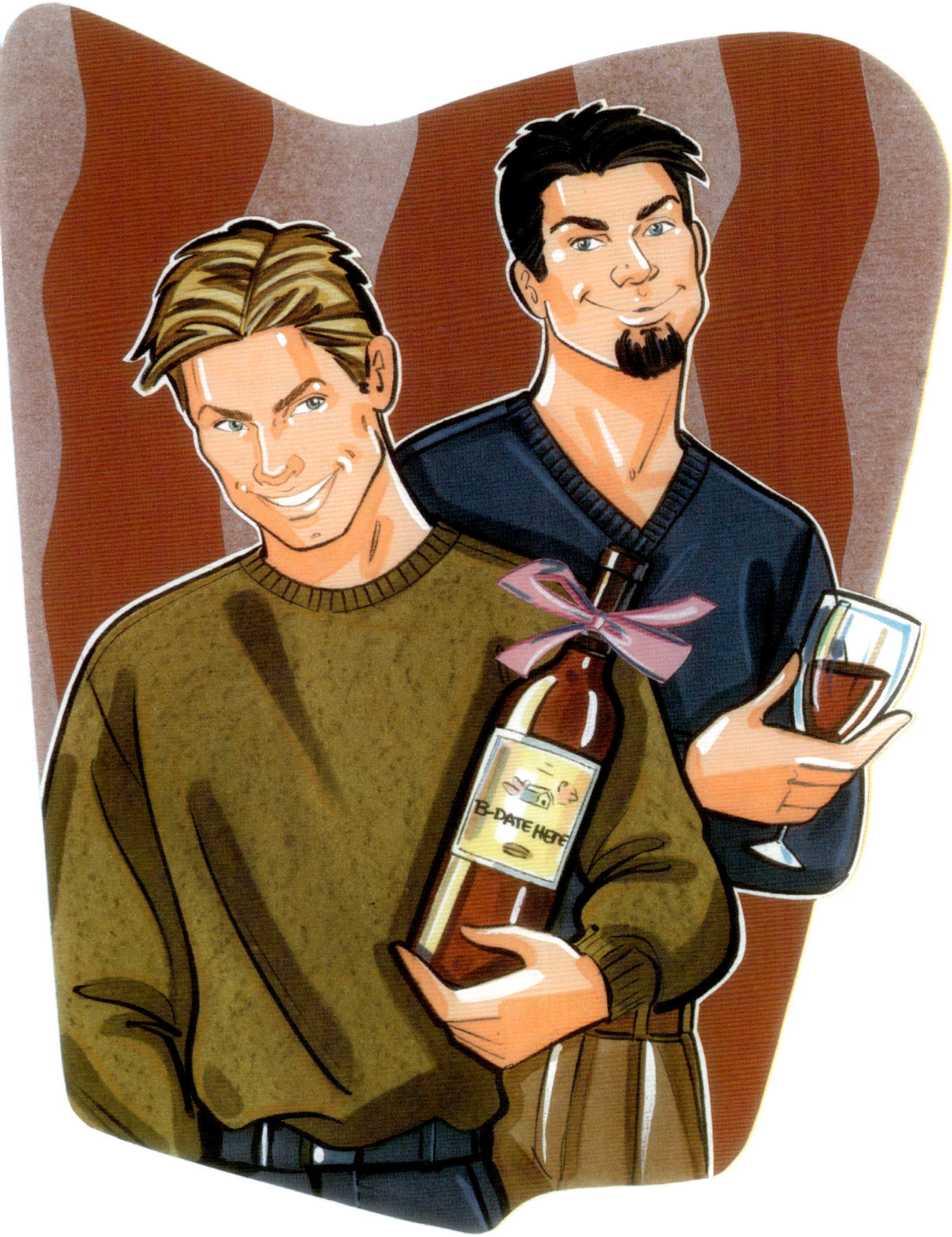
B-DATE HERE

How Could You Forget?

Find a great florist in your neighborhood and let him do all the work. You can preschedule flowers to be delivered for your anniversary, his birthday, Valentine's Day, and any other special day. All that's needed are the dates, occasions, the delivery addresses, and your credit card number. You can even fill out the cards early and have them attached. Then sit back and relax.

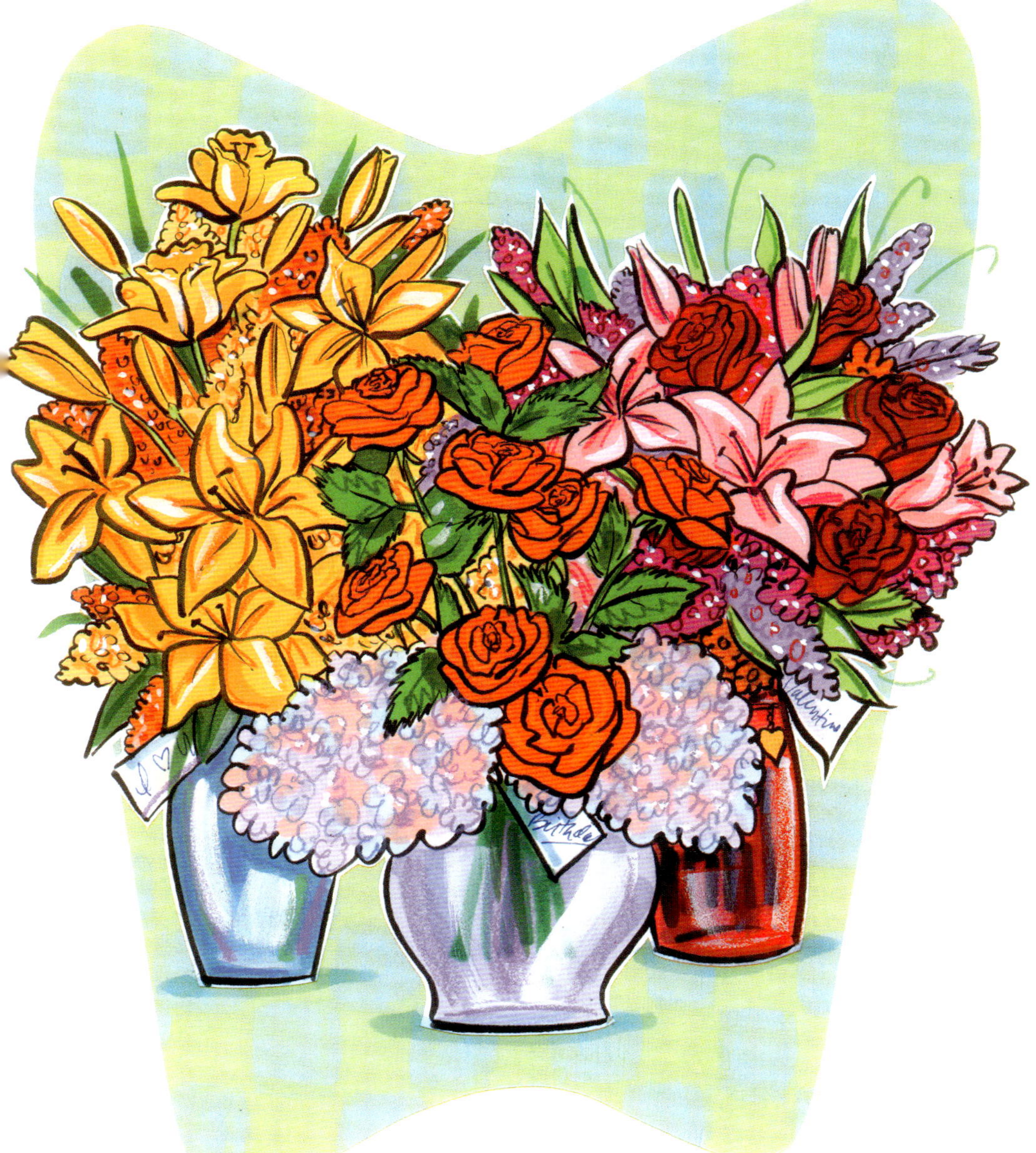

Relax, Just Do It!

Escape from the real world and release your stress together at a beautiful spa. Research them together and choose the one that offers options for both of you—stone rubs, facials, manicures, tennis, room service, you name it.

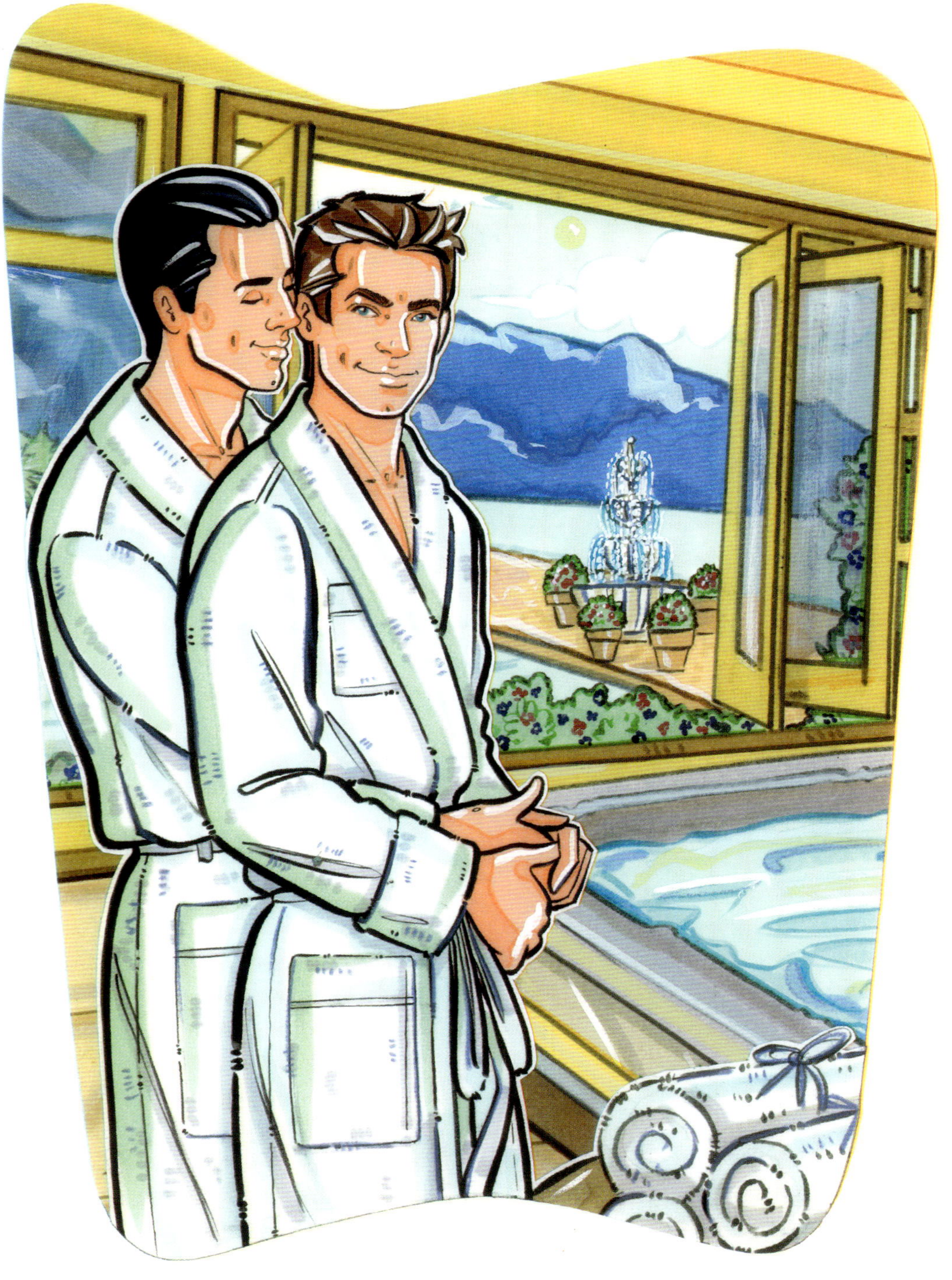

Upside Down, You Turn Me

Celebrate and be proud,
roller coaster style.

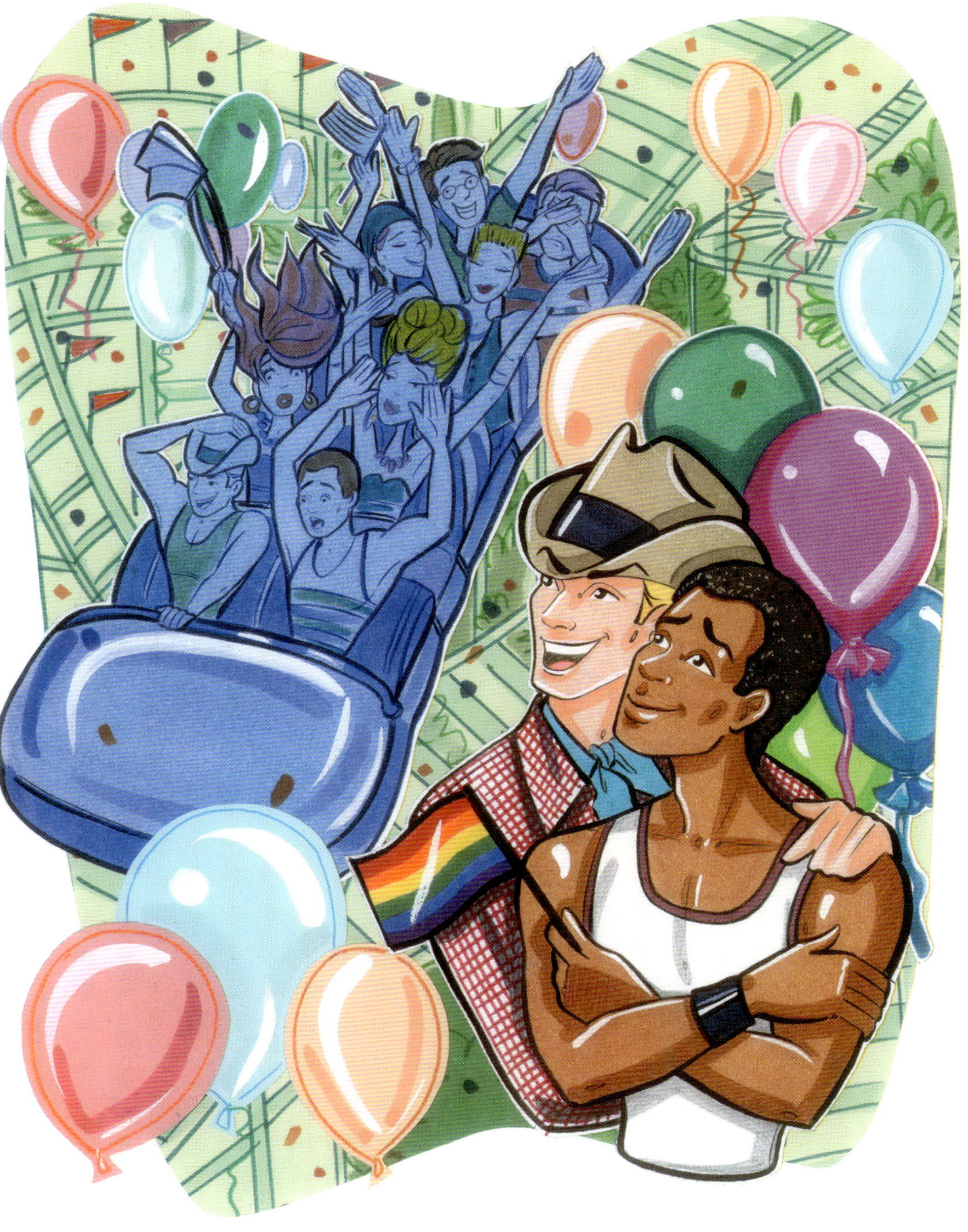

Trick or Treat

This is the one night you can become anything you want. Find an outfit or theme your Romeo finds sexy, then go for it. Top to bottom, you'll be getting into his goodie bag real fast.

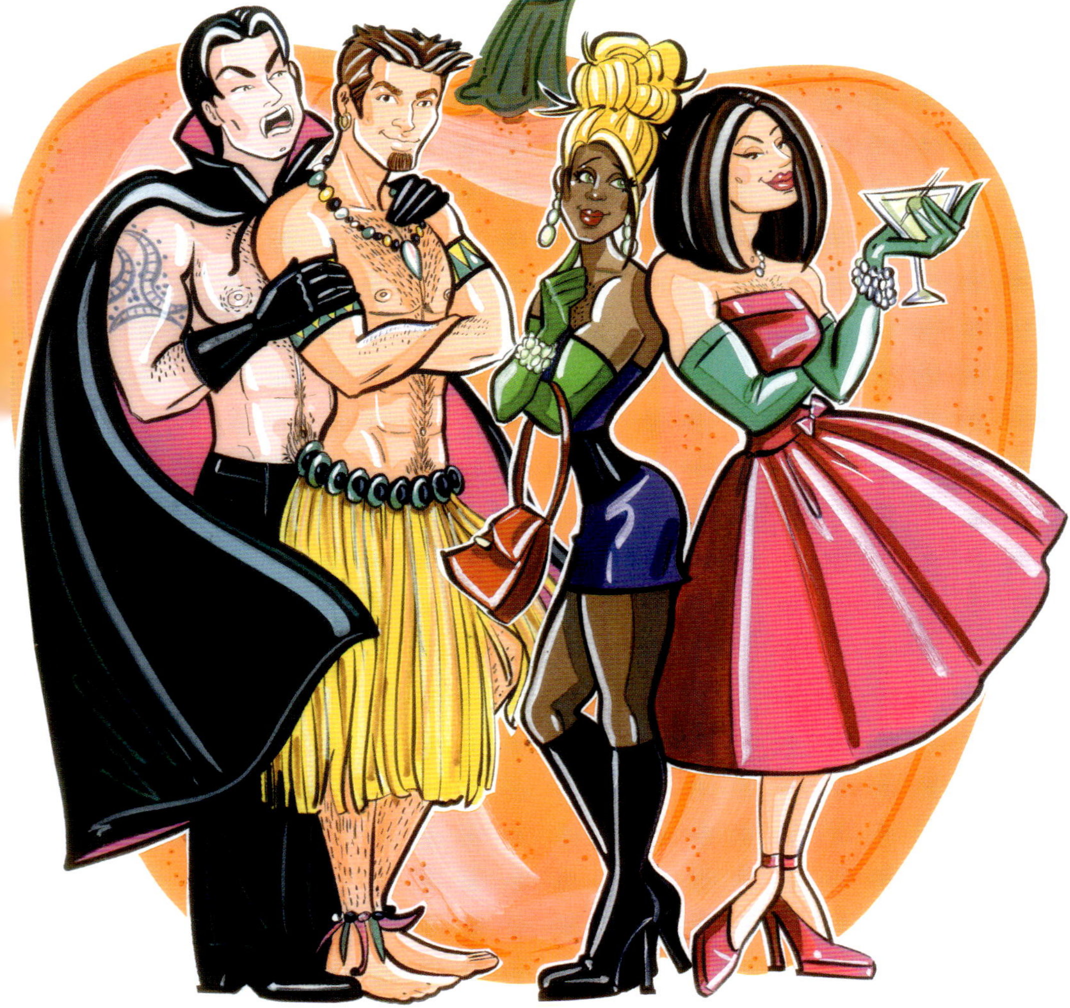

Boner Appétit!

Whipped cream, honey, strawberries, chocolate syrup and cherries are coming out of the fridge and into the bedroom! Dipping them, smearing them and licking them off of your Romeo's different body parts is guaranteed to keep you both from being sex starved.

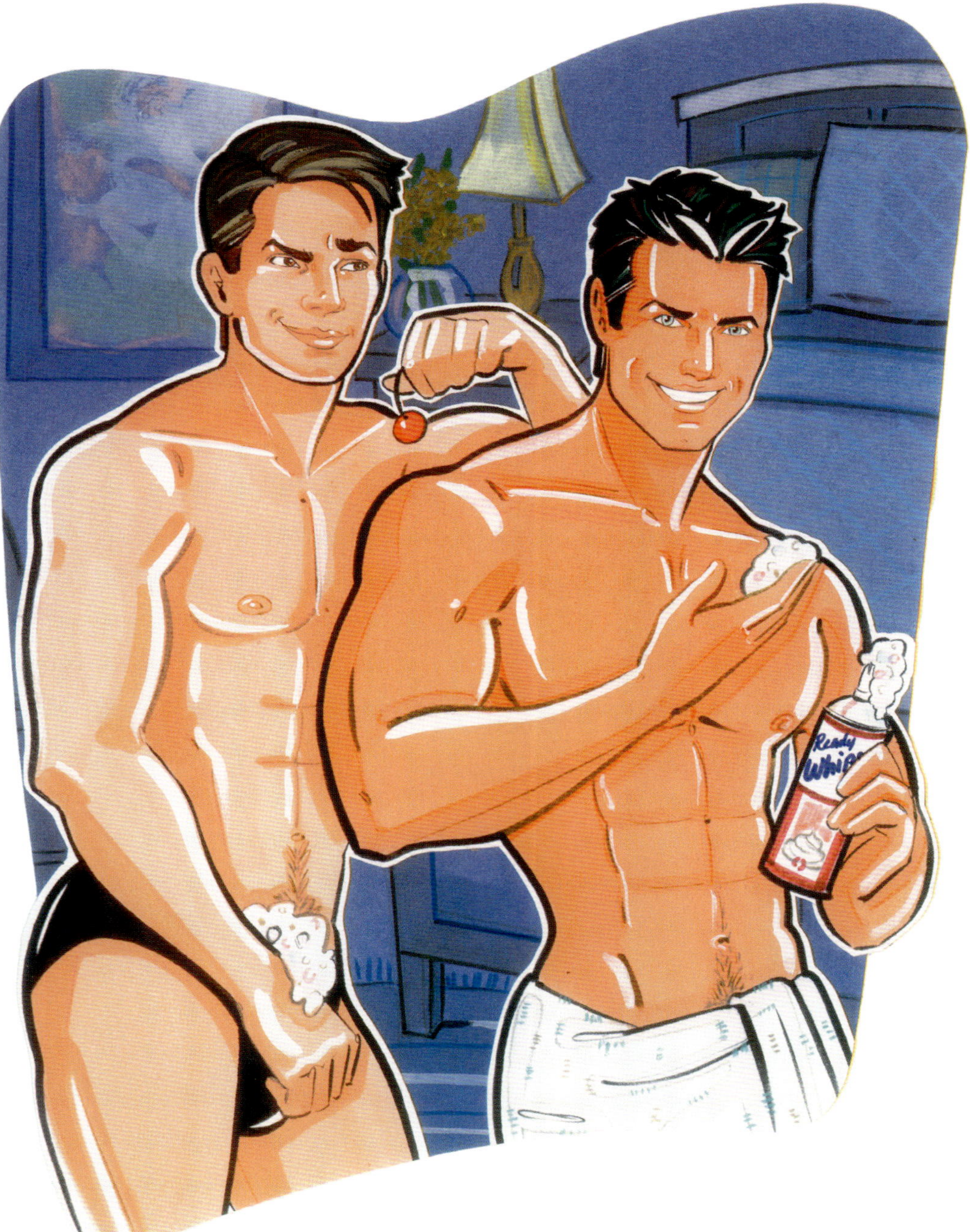
Ready

The Proposal

Coming home from dinner to a house full of candles and flowers (with a little help from a friend), you hand him a balloon bouquet with one of them containing THE RING. Give him a fairy wand with a pin: after he pops the right balloon, the only possible answer is YES!

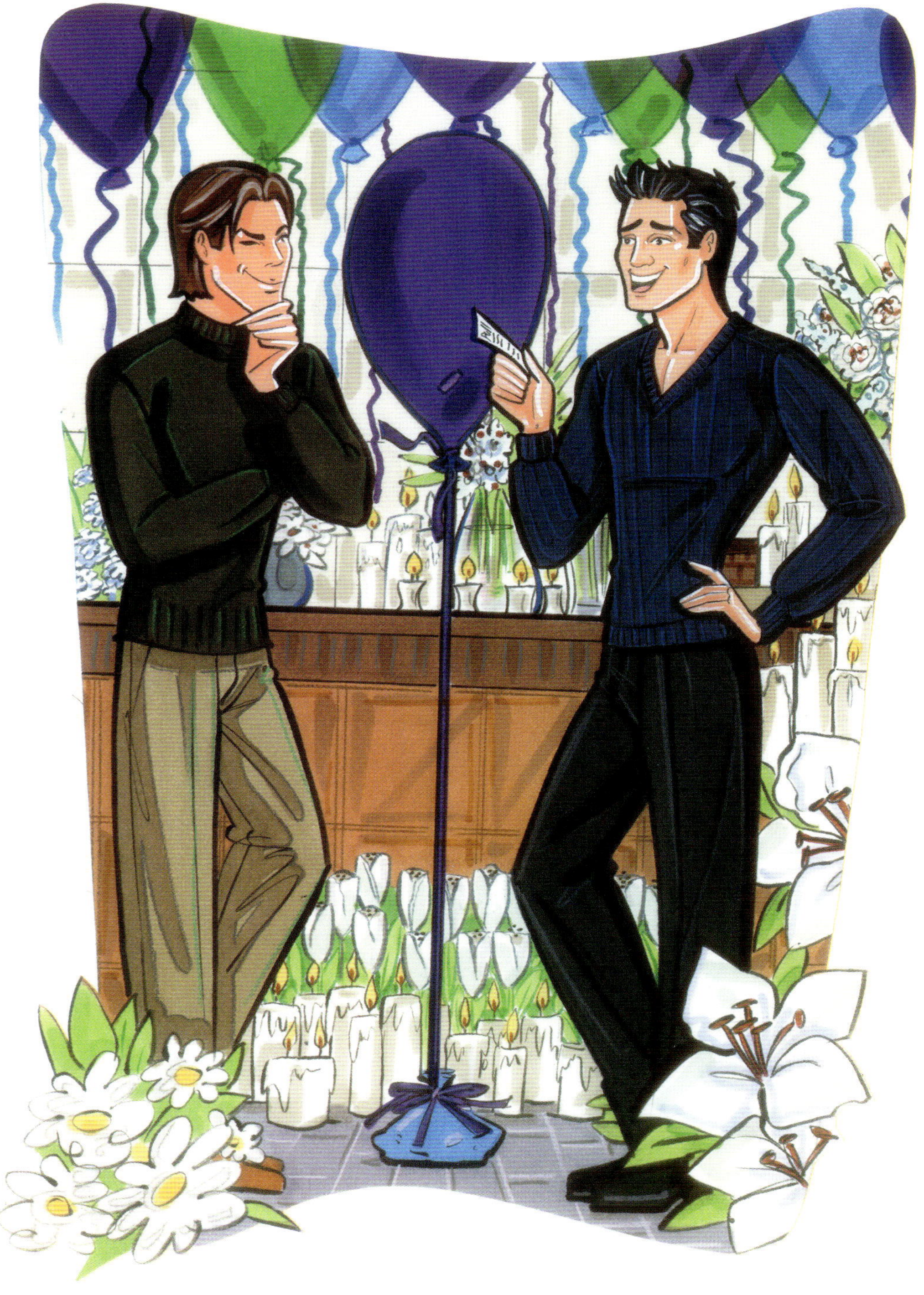

Make His Time Your Time

Give your Romeo the gift of your time. Be aware of special events on his calendar and make yourself available. You'll see the next time you have something important to attend, he'll be right by your side.

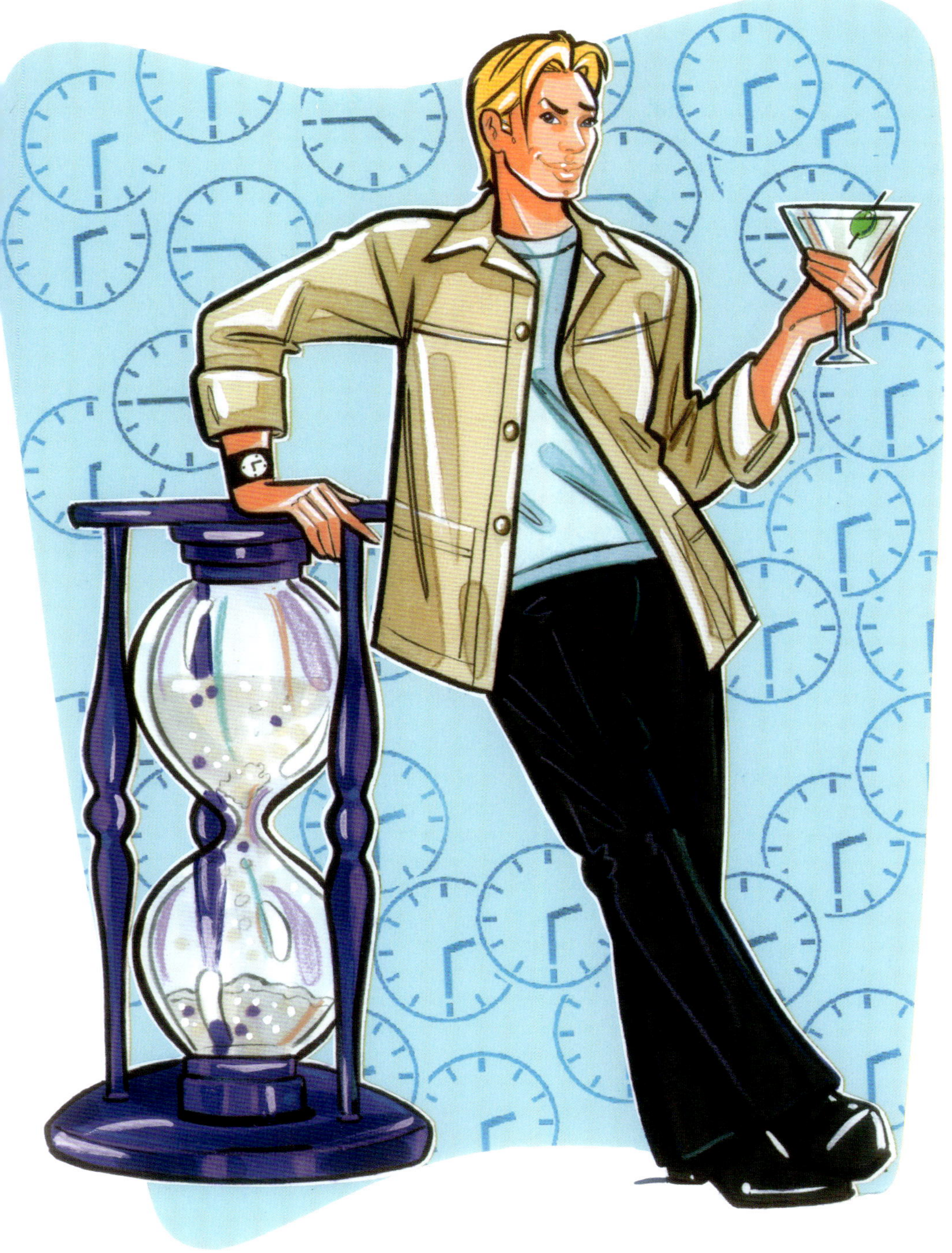

Climbing Partners

Every relationship has its peaks and valleys, its highs and lows. Highs can be moments of sheer ecstasy or high tension. Lows can be peaceful moments of shared intimacy or long, hurtful and uncomfortable silences. Always remember that you are Climbing Partners—navigating your way across new and uncertain terrain, together. Make it a priority to get out your hiking gear and go climbing.

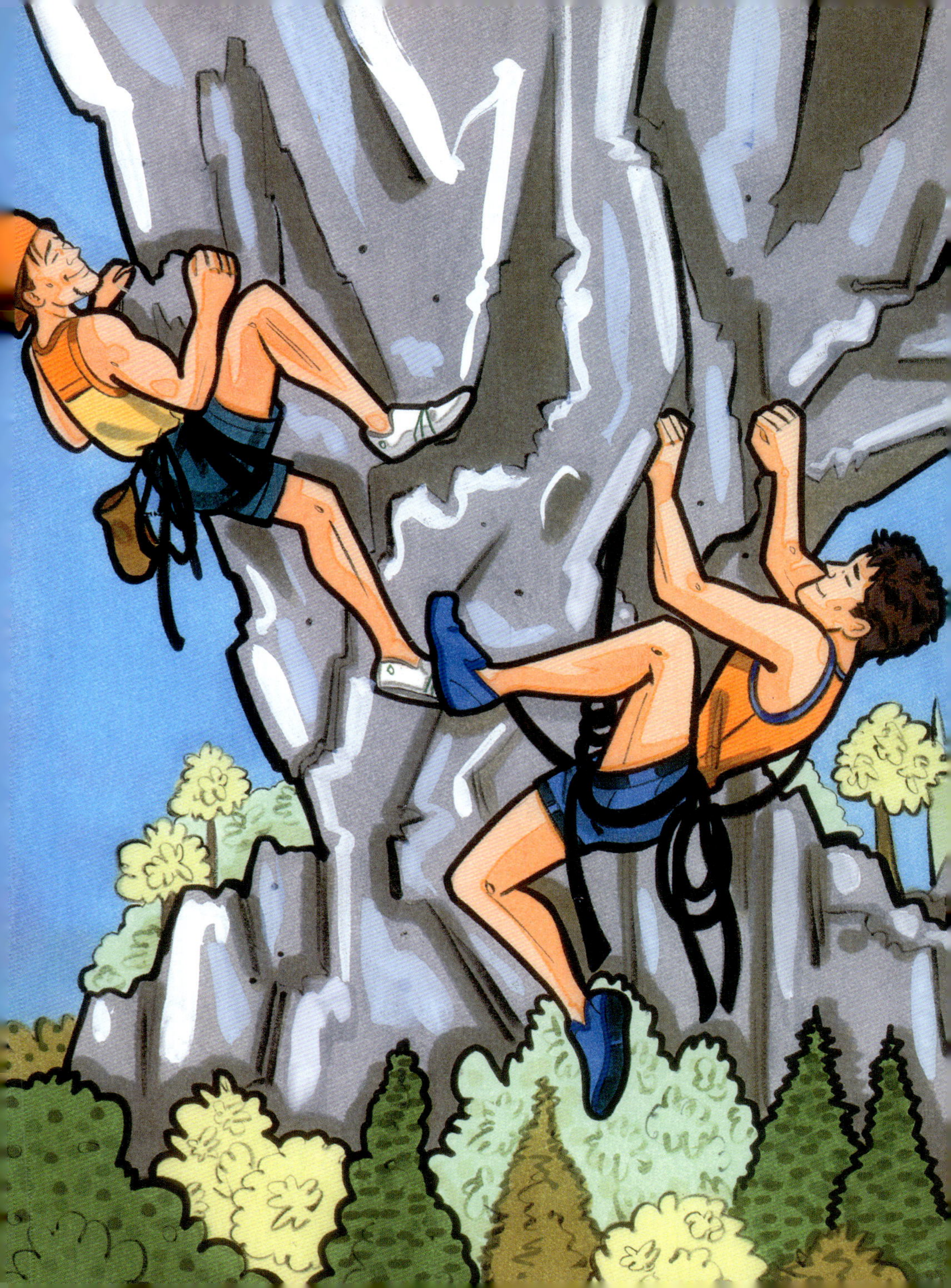

The Firstborn

Nothing says you're ready to share your life with someone better than a puppy. Feeding, nurturing and loving it will bring out all your parental instincts—and take your romance to the next level.

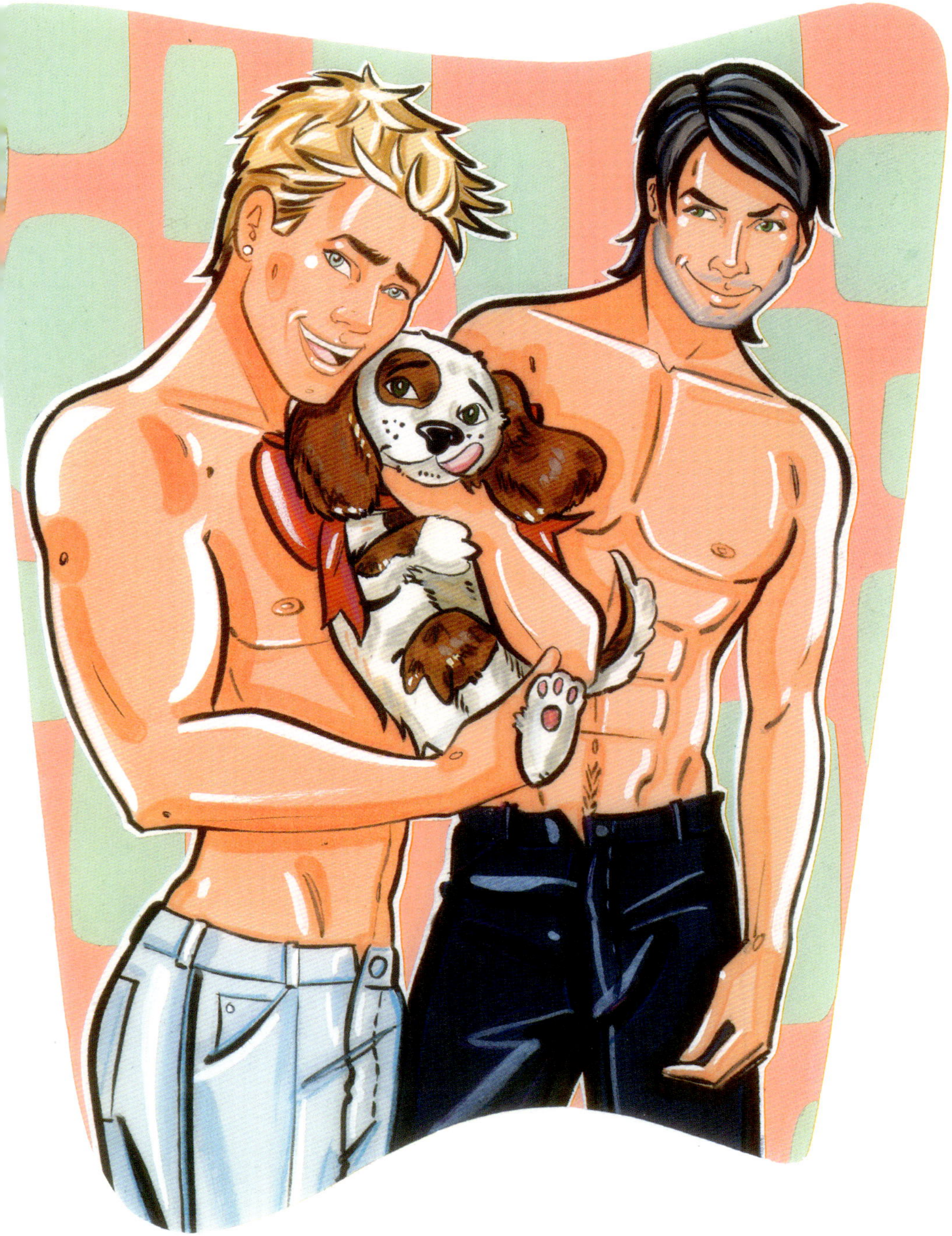

Ding Dong! Romance Calling

Tonight, don't just walk into the house as usual. Pause on the porch, ring the doorbell and greet your man with flowers, a bottle of wine and a big kiss. You'll be his favorite delivery boy in no time.

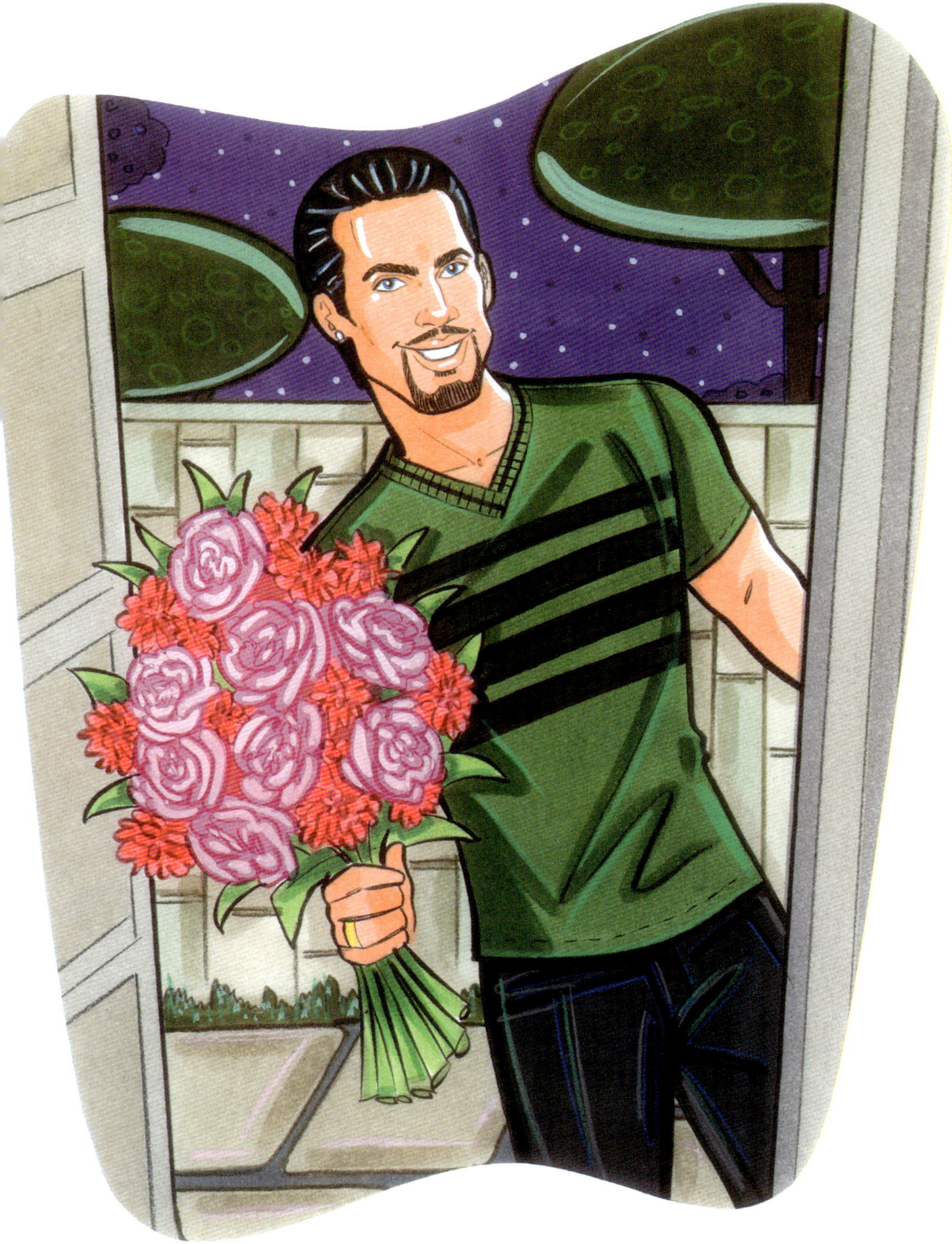

Temperature's Rising!

The next time you are out to dinner together, whether it's at a restaurant, a party, or better yet, a family gathering, whisper in his ear that you aren't wearing any underwear. Then just watch your Romeo heat up.

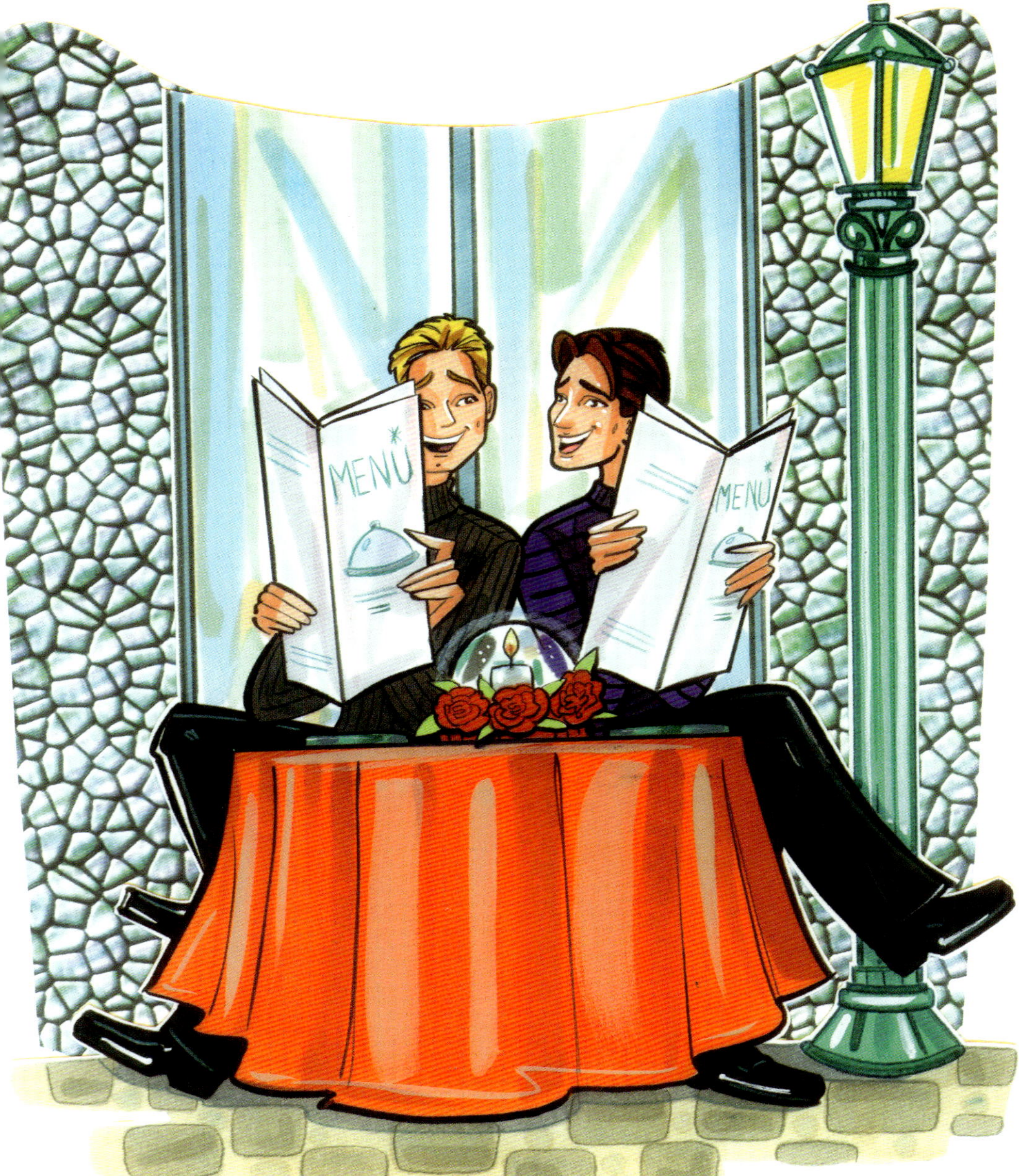
MENU
MENU

The Power of Giving In

It is important to give in to his likes and hobbies now and then—even when you don't share them. Geronimo!

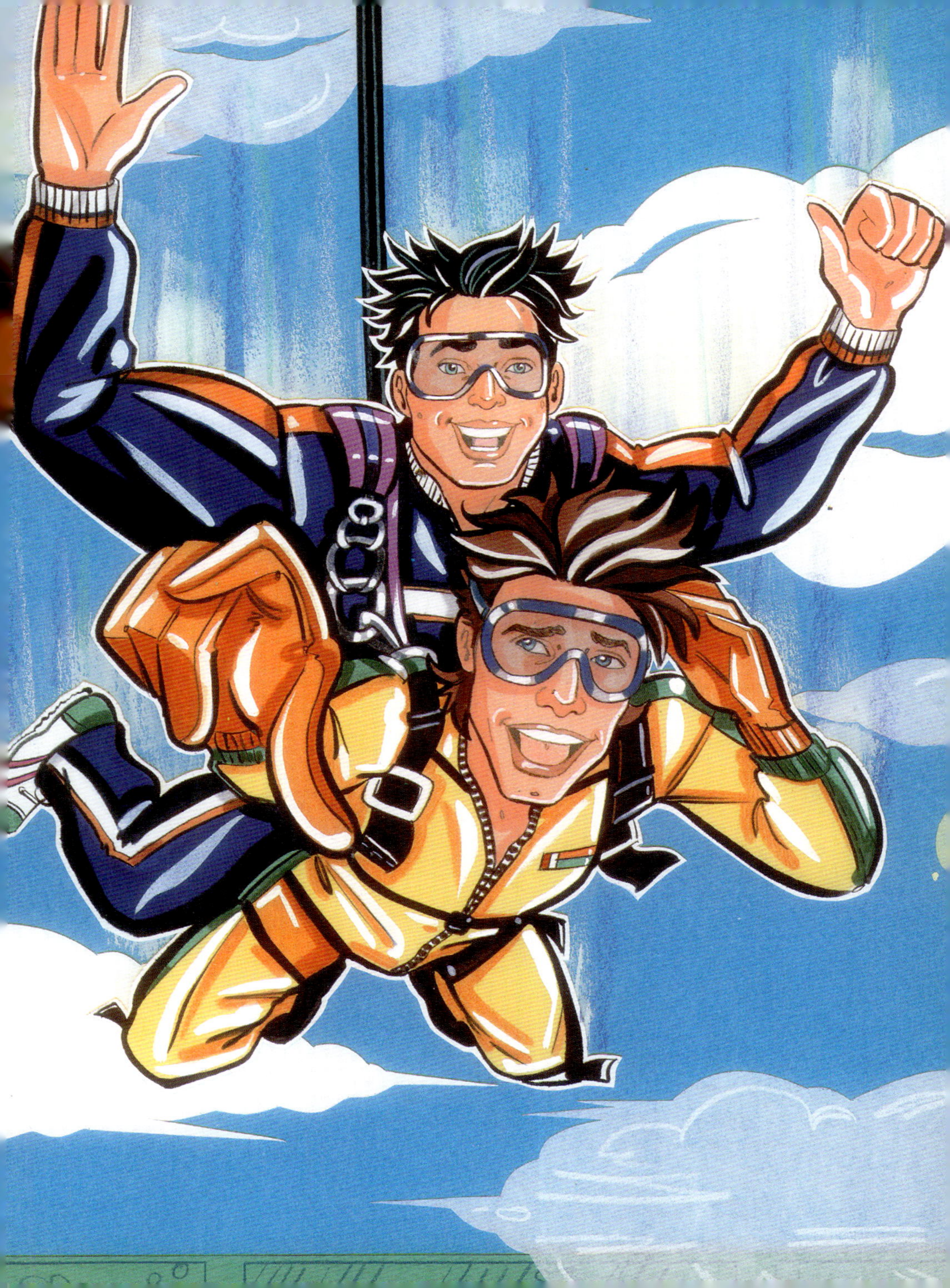

A Novel Idea

Everyone has a favorite book, whether it's by Jules Verne or Julia Child. Find out what his is, then buy a really special copy for him. Try and get the first edition, and if you can get it autographed even better.

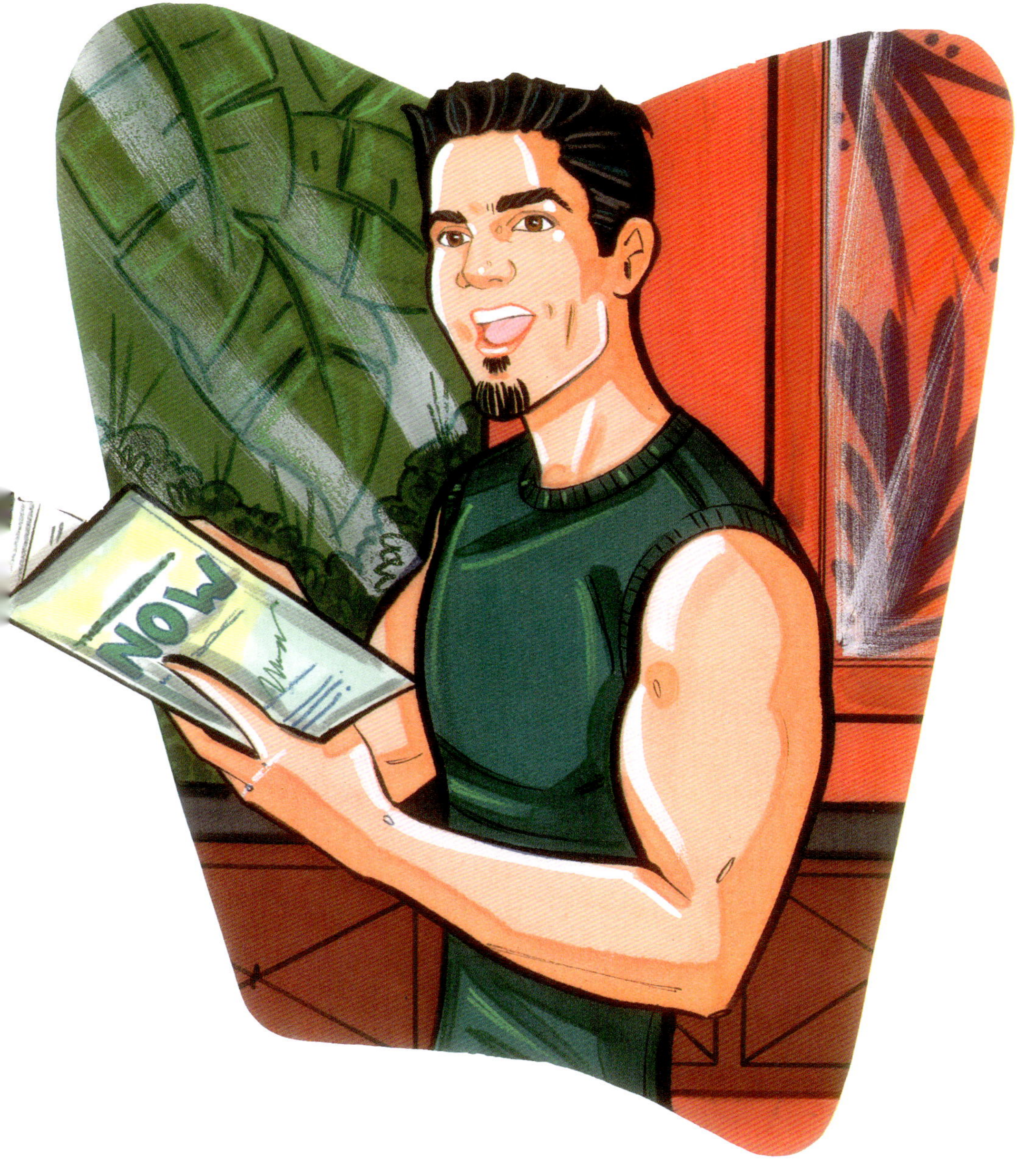
NOW

The Party

This holiday season throw a Clothes for Tots party, where your guests bring new kids' outfits. Then give them to your favorite kids' charity. It's a wonderful gesture and everyone will have fun picking out an outfit.

clothes for Tots

Let it Grow!

Plant a tree in your garden together, and let it represent your relationship. Let the tree's budding and blossoming and growth be a symbol of your strengthening love.

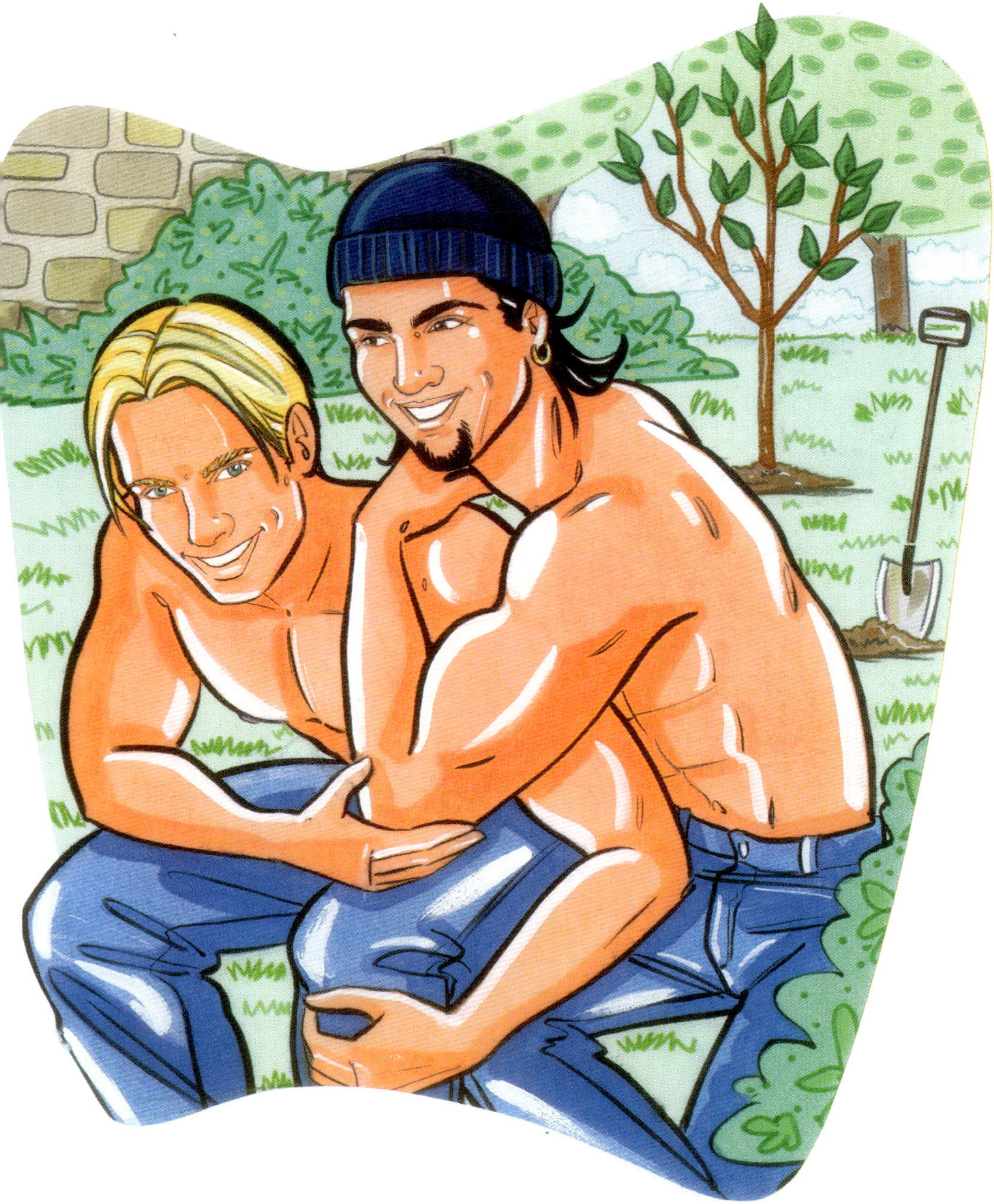

I DO!
The Ceremony

The ultimate fiesta, and the best way to declare your love for each other in front of everyone in your life .

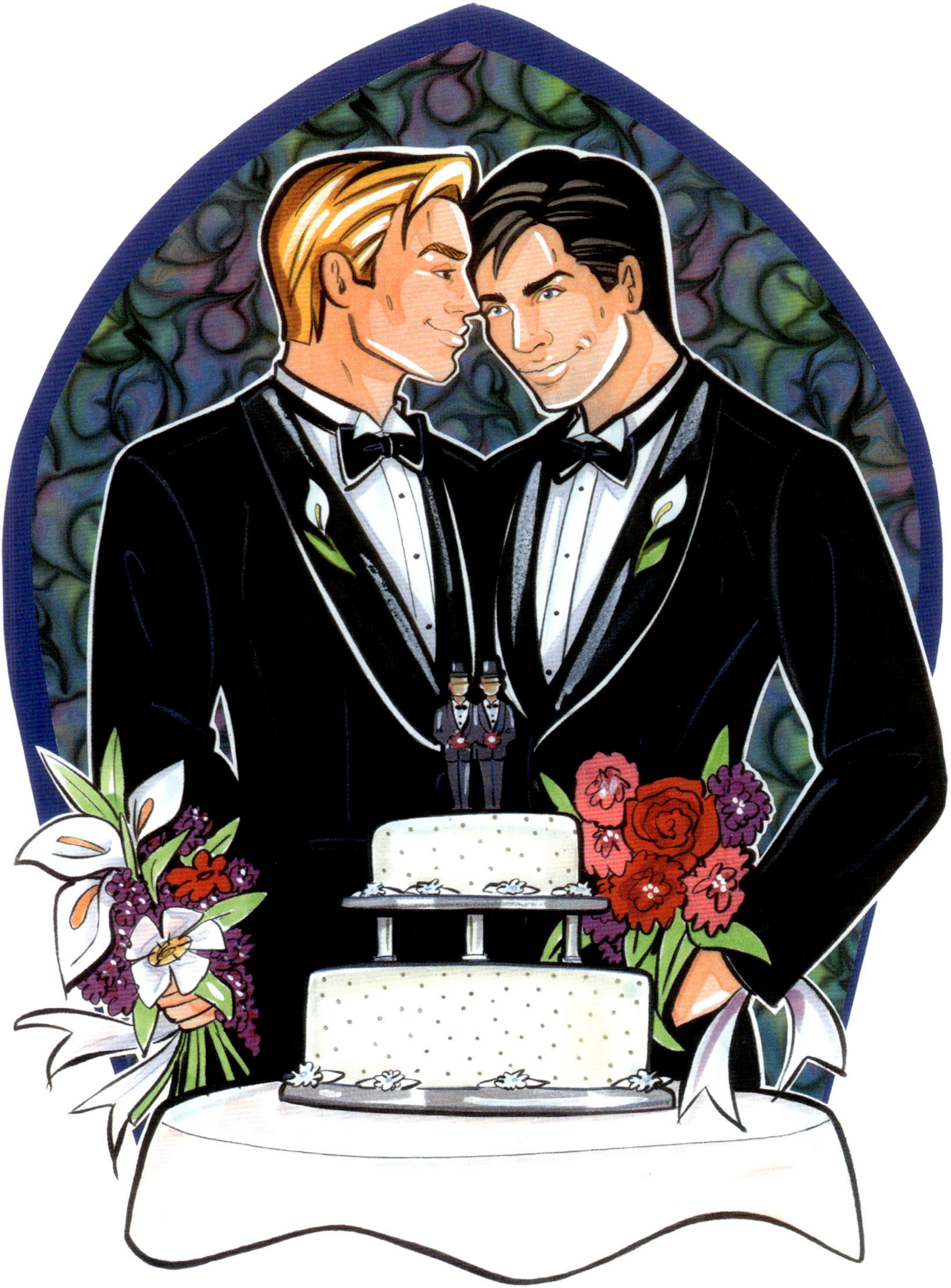

Carlos Marrero's illustrations appear in magazines and newspapers including , *Vogue, Cosmopolitan, Newsweek, The New York Times, Glamour, Mademoiselle, Entertainment Weekly, People, OUT, Genre,* and *The Advocate,* as well as on book covers and calendars. His corporate illustration clients include Helene Curtis, Lancôme, Revlon, L'Oreal, Bloomingdale's, and Abercrombie & Fitch. A graduate of the School of the Art Institute of Chicago, he has taught illustration there as well at Miami Dade Community College and The Art Institute of Fort Lauderdale. His artwork has been showcased in galleries throughout North America including New York, Miami, Chicago, Toronto, Palm Springs, Puerto Rico and San Francisco. Born in Puerto Rico, he now makes his home in Florida and at www.wakeupromeo.com.

♥